Fran

Mary Shelley

Oxford Literature Companions

Notes and activities: Carmel Waldron
Series consultant: Peter Buckroyd

OXFORD
UNIVERSITY PRESS

Contents

What are Oxford Literature Companions?

Oxford Literature Companions is a series designed to provide you with comprehensive support for popular set texts. You can use the Companion alongside your novel, using relevant sections during your studies or using the book as a whole for revision.

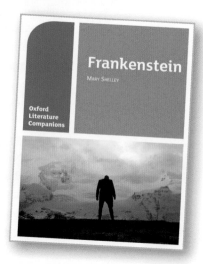

Each Companion includes detailed guidance and practical activities on:

- **Plot and Structure**
- **Context**
- **Characters**
- **Language**
- **Themes**
- **Skills and Practice**

How does this book help with exam preparation?

As well as providing guidance on key areas of the novel, throughout this book you will also find 'Upgrade' features. These are tips to help with your exam preparation and performance.

In addition, in the extensive **Skills and Practice** chapter, the 'Skills for the assessment' section provides detailed guidance on areas such as how to prepare for the exam, understanding the question, planning your response and hints for what to do (or not do) in the exam.

In the **Skills and Practice** chapter there is also a bank of **Sample questions** and **Sample answers**. The **Sample answers** are marked and include annotations and a summative comment.

How does this book help with terminology?

Throughout the book, key terms are **highlighted** in the text and explained on the same page. There is also a detailed **Glossary** at the end of the book that explains, in the context of the novel, all the relevant literary terms highlighted in this book.

Which edition of the novel has this book used?

Quotations and character names have been taken from the Oxford University Press Rollercoaster edition of *Frankenstein* (ISBN 978-0-19-835533-5).

How does this book work?

Each book in the Oxford Literature Companions series follows the same approach and includes the following features:

- **Key quotations** from the novel
- **Key terms** explained on the page and linked to a complete glossary at the end of the book
- **Activity boxes** to help improve your understanding of the text
- **Upgrade** tips to help prepare you for your assessment

Upgrade tips to help prepare you for your assessment

Key quotations from the novel

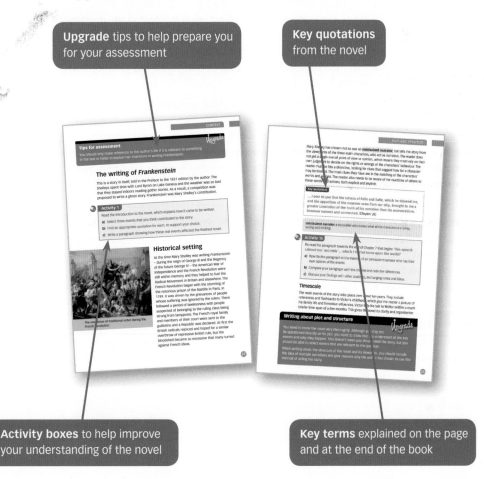

Activity boxes to help improve your understanding of the novel

Key terms explained on the page and at the end of the book

Plot

Introduction and Preface

The Introduction and Preface give an insight into how the story came to be written and how Mary Shelley finally published her 'hideous progeny' (which refers both to the creature and to the novel itself which in a sense is 'stitched together' from different narratives). The story itself is famous, but readers are often surprised when they read the original book at how different it is from what they already know.

The novel then begins with letters from a Robert Walton to his sister Margaret Saville. Within the letters he recounts a story told to him by a stranger he rescues from the icy seas.

Letters 1–4

Written from St Petersburg in December, these first letters tell of Walton's determination to find the North Pole. He describes his great interest in the mystery of the magnetic pole, the lure of undiscovered lands and his fascination with 'celestial observation'. The reader also learns that he inherited a fortune on his cousin's death which has enabled him to fund his expedition. His preparation for the journey, both physical and intellectual has been thorough.

By the following March Walton has reached **Archangel**, where he hires a ship and a crew but laments that he does not have a true friend to travel with him. The ship's master is described as a noble and beloved man but uneducated and taciturn. Walton quotes from **_The Rime of the Ancient Mariner_** and tells his sister that this poem fed his desire to see the Arctic. In July Walton's ship is under way, they have met with no mishaps and he is confident of achieving his goal.

By August they are left stranded among plains of ice. One day they see a gigantic man driving a dog carriage across the ice. Later they rescue a man from a similar carriage that has drifted off on an **ice floe** drowning most of the dogs. They take pains to revive this man and restore him to health. He becomes excited to hear of their previous sighting and Robert Walton feels kinship and sympathy with him, as a man of education and cultivated manners. When Walton tells him of his obsession

---

Key quotations

What may not be expected in a country of eternal light? *(Letter 1)*

Archangel a northern port of Russia, at the entrance to the White Sea

ice floe a large piece of ice that moves freely with the current

The Rime of the Ancient Mariner a long narrative poem by Samuel Taylor Coleridge in which the Mariner travels to the North Pole and is cursed for killing an albatross

with reaching the North Pole, the man, who is Victor Frankenstein, tells his own story as a warning against too much ambition. Walton claims to have written the story word for word as Frankenstein told it to him.

- Walton's determination and ambition mirror Frankenstein's – a focus of both narratives.
- Walton's story frames the narrative of Frankenstein's, starting at the point where Victor's ends.
- In another parallel, the two men are both alone without family or friends.

Activity 1

What are your impressions of Robert Walton from his letters? Think about:

- his reliability as a narrator
- his personality and upbringing
- his relationship with his sister
- his relationship with his crew
- his reactions to Frankenstein.

Make notes on your ideas.

Chapters 1 and 2

We discover that Victor Frankenstein was born in Naples, but has Swiss nationality. His father was married late in life to Caroline Beaufort, the daughter of an old friend whom he rescued from dire poverty after the death of her father. When Victor was five the family visited Lake Como where they helped to ease poverty and suffering. On one visit to a poor family his mother found a small blonde girl she took a fancy to. She brought the girl back to be cared for alongside Victor. Her name was Elizabeth Lavenza and everyone loved her.

Seven years later, after the birth of his younger brother Ernest, the Frankenstein family settled in Geneva. Victor went to school but was a solitary boy who made few friends other than Henry Clerval. Clerval was a romantic youth who wanted to imitate the exploits of the heroes of medieval chivalry. Any excessive rowdiness by the two boys was calmed by Elizabeth, the guiding spirit.

Victor discovered the occult sciences through studying **Cornelius Agrippa**, **Paracelcus** and **Albertus Magnus**. These works led him to explore the mysteries of the Philosopher's Stone and the Elixir of Life. He dreamed of banishing disease and illness from human life. The heady mix of magic and science enthralled Victor until he discovered a new enthusiasm. One day he witnessed an oak tree being destroyed

Cornelius Agrippa, Paracelcus, Albertus Magnus medieval philosophers and alchemists

in a lightning storm. A visitor staying with the family was a specialist in **Natural Philosophy**, researching **galvanism** and electricity. His instruction destroyed Victor's faith in occult science and made him turn to Mathematics instead.

- The story of Elizabeth will have an echo in the story of Justine Moritz, later.
- The introduction of Henry Clerval as Victor's only friend becomes important further on.
- The influence of his reading and his father's friend have implications for Victor in his later studies.

> **Key quotations**
>
> Wealth was an inferior object; but what glory would attend the discovery, if I could banish disease from the human frame, and render man invulnerable to any but a violent death! *(Chapter 2)*

Activity 2

In Chapter 1 Victor says of his father, 'the circumstances of his marriage illustrate his character'.

a) Rewrite the story of Victor's parents in five sentences.

b) Use bullet points to give your views on what their story tells the reader about Alphonse Frankenstein.

c) Find three quotations that suggest the character of Victor's mother.

Chapters 3 and 4

Victor is to continue his education at the University of Ingolstadt, but Elizabeth becomes ill with **scarlet fever**. In nursing her back to health, Victor's mother catches the illness and dies. On her deathbed she joins the hands of Victor and Elizabeth, urging them to marry when they are ready. After a period of mourning and a final night spent with his father and Henry Clerval, Victor sets off for Ingolstadt. Clerval's father refuses to allow him to attend university, wanting him to go into the family business, against Clerval's own wishes.

When Victor arrives and meets his professors, he dislikes the professor of Natural Philosophy, Mr Krempe, who sneers at his previous reading, but likes the Chemistry professor, Mr Waldman. These two subjects fill his time and he studies them eagerly. He is filled with grand ideas about furthering the course of Natural Philosophy to 'unfold to the world the deepest mysteries of creation'.

After two years of hard study Victor has learned all he can from his professors about Natural Philosophy. He becomes obsessed with finding the origin of life and initially devotes his time to studying the processes of death and decay. He spends his time in graveyards and **charnel houses**, observing corpses at all stages of decomposition.

Then he has a breakthrough moment of inspiration, which reveals the source of life. He devotes every moment to creating a human being. He is possessed by this one objective, excluding everything else. He assembles all the parts he needs and experiments on them in his rooms. The microscopic nature of the work leads him to decide to make his creature about eight feet tall and in proportion.

- His mother's death is Victor's first experience of losing a loved one and influences his eventual decision about his life's work.

- Clerval's inability to accompany Victor to Ingolstadt prevents him acting as a brake on Frankenstein's wild ideas.

- The subjects Victor studies feed his imagination and his intellect, which outstrips that of his professors.

- Mary Shelley sets the scene for the ultimate creation of a being through the horrors of graveyards and decaying corpses.

> **Key quotations**
>
> **Pursuing these reflections, I thought, that if I could bestow animation upon lifeless matter, I might in process of time (although I now found it impossible) renew life where death had apparently devoted the body to corruption.** *(Chapter 4)*

Activity 3

1. Re-read from paragraph 2 in Chapter 4, starting **'One of the phenomena ...'** to '... **discover so astonishing a secret'**.

   a) Find two phrases that tell the reader Frankenstein's character was equal to the task of studying death and decay.

   b) Find two phrases that suggest the horror most people would feel in his situation.

   c) Find two phrases that show the amazement Victor feels at his breakthrough.

2. Based on this evidence, write a paragraph about Mary Shelley's techniques for creating contrasting emotions in her readers.

charnel house originally a storage chamber for bones at the time when graves were re-used; generally a place of death and decay

galvanism named after Galvani, a scientist who discovered the effect of electric current on dead limbs

Natural Philosophy the study of Nature through science that preceded modern natural sciences

scarlet fever an infectious illness that mainly affects children and killed many in the days before antibiotics

Chapters 5 and 6

'It was on a dreary night in November, that I beheld the accomplishment of my toils.' *(Chapter 5)* Frankenstein gathers 'the instruments of life' and animates his assembled creation. As soon as it opens its eyes, he is horrified by it and runs away to his room. When he sleeps, he dreams of meeting Elizabeth in Ingolstadt and embracing her, but she changes into his mother's corpse. He wakes to find the creature by his bed, grinning and reaching out to him. Rejecting it in terror, Victor flees into the courtyard of the house where he passes a disturbed night. The next morning he walks through the town and bumps into Clerval, who has just arrived, having persuaded his father to let him come. Victor's behaviour is manic and worries his friend. Victor succumbs to a life-threatening illness and fever, which the devoted Clerval nurses him through.

Kenneth Branagh's Frankenstein assembles his creature, played by Robert De Niro, in the 1994 film *Mary Shelley's Frankenstein*

As Victor recovers his health, Clerval gives him a letter from Elizabeth. Victor's family are anxious about him because they've heard nothing from him. Elizabeth gives news of his family and of Justine Moritz. She had been taken on as a servant by Victor's mother, who worried that the girl's own mother neglected her. Justine became devoted to Mrs Frankenstein and nursed her through her final illness. Wrapped up in their own grief, the family failed to consider Justine, who became ill. Justine's mother lost all her own family, thought the illness was a judgment on her behaviour to Justine and insisted that the girl came home. When her mother died, Justine returned to the Frankensteins and was happy. Elizabeth also comments on Victor's youngest brother William and how attractive he is.

Victor recovers his health but is nervous and unable to bear any mention of Natural Philosophy or to have anything to do with his former occupation. He doesn't tell Clerval about the creature but keeps his creation secret. Instead he joins Clerval in studying Oriental Languages. Before returning to Geneva, Victor and Henry go on a walking holiday and Frankenstein regains his former joy in life.

- Victor's total rejection of the creature he has made and his refusal to take responsibility for it drives the rest of the story.
- The arrival of Clerval reminds him of life before his obsession with creating a human being and his illness is a symptom of his guilt.
- The story of Justine and the mention of William in Elizabeth's letter foreshadow the deaths that happen later.

> **Key quotations**
>
> ... I beheld the wretch – the miserable monster whom I had created. *(Chapter 5)*

Activity 4

The first paragraph of Chapter 5 describes the animation of the creature.

a) Discuss or consider how Mary Shelley creates the atmosphere of doom that surrounds the creature's 'birth'. You should think about:

- how she uses the weather outside
- how she uses the lighting inside
- the words she uses to describe the creature stirring into life.

b) Write a paragraph about Shelley's use of words and symbols (e.g. the dying candle) to make the reader aware of Frankenstein's dreadful mistake.

Chapters 7 and 8

Victor receives a letter from his father, which tells him his brother William is dead. He had been playing with his brother Ernest, had gone to hide and could not be found. Later, his body was found strangled. Elizabeth, suspecting robbery as the murderer's motive, blamed herself for allowing him to wear a valuable miniature of his mother, which was missing. His father begs Victor to come home and console Elizabeth. Clerval's sympathy is a consolation to Victor, but he hurries home, breaking his journey at Lausanne. When he arrives at Geneva after sunset the town is closed, so he has to spend the night at a nearby village.

Unable to sleep, Victor visits the site of William's murder, taking a boat across the lake. He admires the storm lightning playing across Mont Blanc. When he arrives at the place the lightning reveals the figure of 'the wretch, the filthy daemon, to whom I had given life'. Victor is convinced that his creature is William's murderer.

daemon originally a nature spirit, it later became a name for an evil spirit

At first he wants to tell the authorities, but then reflects that his story would sound like the ravings of a madman. When Ernest says that Justine Moritz has been arrested for the murder, Victor is horrified and tells his family of her innocence, but without mentioning his creature. His father reassures him that he can rely on the laws of Switzerland to acquit her if she is not guilty.

Justine Moritz is tried for William's murder and found guilty. Elizabeth is one of the few who defend her, but the court's sympathy is against Justine, who cannot explain how the valuable miniature came into her possession. They do not believe her explanation that she went to visit an aunt, heard of the child's disappearance and was looking for him when she was locked out of the city and spent the night in a barn. Victor is so upset that he hurries from the courtroom.

Victor returns the next morning intending to tell what he knows about the creature. He is met with the news that Justine has confessed and hurries home to tell Elizabeth. When they go to see Justine she tells them the priest threatened her with eternal damnation if she did not confess. Her 'confession' means a death sentence, which fills Victor with grief and guilt. He and Elizabeth appeal to the judges but, when he hears their words, Victor fails to tell them of the creature, assuming they will dismiss him as a madman. Justine is executed and Victor bemoans his deed in creating the killer of William and Justine, and bringing misery to those he loves.

- Having abandoned his responsibility towards the creature, Victor now abandons responsibility for its actions and allows Justine to die.
- Victor's father represents all those citizens who put their faith in those in authority – in this case the justice system – with fatal results.
- Justine and William become the first victims of the creature's desire for revenge.

Key quotations

Did anyone indeed exist, except I, the creator, who would believe, unless his senses convinced him, in the existence of the living monument of presumption and rash ignorance which I had let loose upon the world? *(Chapter 7)*

Activity 5

Think about why Mary Shelley made Justine Moritz the victim of injustice:

a) to show the unfairness of the justice system of her day – run only by men

b) to show the oppression of a male-dominated religion

c) to demonstrate the way even the best person can be turned upon by society

d) to reveal Victor's cowardly behaviour.

Make notes on your opinions, supported by quotations. Compare your answers with other students' opinions and amend them if you wish.

Chapters 9 and 10

Once more Victor lapses into nervous ill health, tormented by his conscience. His father moves the family to their country house at Belrive where Victor wanders by the lake and contemplates suicide. He refrains from this drastic step for the sake of Elizabeth and his family. He is racked with remorse, fear that the creature might appear and a desire for revenge on his creation. Elizabeth urges him to put aside the dark feelings she sees in him, but Victor leaves home and travels to Chamonix, hoping to find peace in the magnificent scenery around Mont Blanc.

On his first day in Chamonix, Victor's nerves are soothed by the wonder of Nature as he wanders the valley. The following morning he wakes, depressed again, to pouring rain. He sets out on his mule to get to the summit of Montanvert. It is noon before he arrives and he descends to the glacier, which takes him two hours to cross. Victor sees a man bounding towards him over the ice and realizes it is the creature. He is overcome with rage and hatred. He makes threats to the creature and tries to attack it. The creature replies to his insults in a voice of reason and eloquence, and appeals to Victor as his creator who has abandoned him. He asks Victor to listen to him. The creature leads Victor to a hut with a fire and begins his tale.

- Victor's illnesses appear to be the symptoms of a guilty conscience and may be a form of denial of responsibility.
- Nature has a profound effect on his moods and feelings.
- The first meeting between creator and creature since its animation is on an ice plain, which foreshadows the Arctic wastes of the final scenes.

Key quotations

Remember, that I am thy creature; I ought to be thy Adam; but I am rather the fallen angel, whom thou drivest from joy for no misdeed. *(Chapter 10)*

Activity 6

1. Re-read paragraphs 4 and 5 of Chapter 10.

   a) Write down three phrases that describe Victor's first impression of the creature.

   b) Write down three phrases that describe Victor's reaction when he realizes he has seen the creature.

   c) In your own words, write down Victor's 'greeting' to the creature.

   d) In your own words, write down the creature's reply.

2. Discuss or consider what this unexpected meeting reveals of the way these two think and feel about each other.

Chapters 11 and 12

The creature relates how he came to life and learned to distinguish day and night, heat and cold, light and dark. He had a few clothes from Frankenstein's apartment and found a cloak in the woods, where he went for shelter. One day he found a fire and, feeling its warmth, put his hand into it. He was very surprised that the same source could provide both pleasure and pain. He travelled further to look for food and shelter but was greeted with fear and aggression by the humans he encountered. At last he found a wooden outhouse adjoining a cottage which was dry and where he would not be seen.

The creature followed the life of the De Lacey family in the cottage – an old man, a girl and a boy (Agatha and Felix). He felt unusual emotions as he watched the relationships of these three and their affection for each other. He observed the kindly way the family behaved, in particular to the blind father, but also their sadness, which stemmed from poverty. When he realized they didn't have enough to eat, he stopped stealing food from them and lived on berries and tubers foraged from the woods.

The creature discovered human speech and applied himself to the task of acquiring language. He noticed words produced emotions in the hearers and shared the family's feelings. The creature admired the family's good looks and was terrified and depressed when he saw his own reflection in a pool. He helped them by doing work for the cottage and, when he heard the family refer to their 'good spirit', he dreamed of winning their affection.

- The creature's development follows that of a human but without guidance from a parent.
- He learns how his appearance makes him an outcast and repulsive to humans.
- The De Lacey family provide an example of family life he can never have.

> **Key quotations**
>
> **I had admired the perfect forms of my cottagers – their grace, beauty and delicate complexions: but how was I terrified, when I viewed myself in a transparent pool!** *(Chapter 12)*

Activity 7

1. The first seven paragraphs of Chapter 11 tell of the creature's development and learning.

   a) Make a list of all the sensations and impressions the creature mentions.

   b) Write three sentences about his discovery of fire and its uses and problems.

2. Later in the chapter the creature encounters people. Describe two events that make the creature aware he is not welcome in human society.

Chapters 13 and 14

The creature had noticed Felix was melancholy but didn't know why. Then a stranger – a beautiful woman called Safie – arrived and transformed Felix. He called her his 'sweet Arabian' and the family welcomed her. It seemed she could not understand their language, nor they hers. Agatha taught Safie to speak their language while Felix taught her to write. The creature learned at the same time. He used a book about world history and empires called **Ruins of Empire** by Volney. This made the creature think about the state of humanity, which he sees as 'at once so powerful, so virtuous and magnificent yet so vicious and base'. He also learned about society and its divisions by birth and wealth. He cannot see where he fits into this order and wonders if he is 'a monster, a blot upon the earth, from which all men fled, and whom all men disowned'. The creature learned about parents and families but realized he has none and asked 'What was I?'

The creature learned the family's history, discovering their name was De Lacey and that they had been a well-off family in Paris until Safie's father ruined them. He was a Turkish merchant who had been condemned to death on a false charge. Felix had visited him and made plans for his escape and had also seen and fallen for Safie. Her father promised her hand in marriage when he gained his freedom and Felix smuggled the two of them to Italy. Safie's mother was a Christian Arab taken as a slave by the Turks until she married Safie's father. She brought up Safie in her religion and the principles of freedom, which made the girl unwilling to spend her life in a Turkish harem. When their plot was discovered, Agatha and her father were imprisoned, causing Felix to return to them, leaving Safie and her father. The De Laceys were exiled from France and lost all their wealth. When the merchant found out he reneged on his promise and ordered Safie to follow him as he fled back to Constantinople. Instead Safie finds Felix's address in her father's papers and journeys to find him.

- The creature's education from the De Lacey family shows the ideal of family and social life, which he can never experience, as well as the importance placed on birth and wealth.
- Felix's book, from which the creature learns, shows the greatness and baseness of human beings throughout history, while the De Laceys' own story provides a practical and intimate example of this.
- The resourceful Safie contrasts to the passivity of the females in Victor's family.

> **Key quotations**
>
> For a long time I could not conceive how one man could go forth to murder his fellow, or even why there were laws and governments; but when I heard details of vice and bloodshed, my wonder ceased, and I turned away with disgust and loathing. *(Chapter 13)*

Ruins of Empire the central theme of this book by Volney is that empires rise when government allows enlightened self-interest to flourish

Activity 8

The creature says **"I learned that the possessions most esteemed by your fellow-creatures were, high and unsullied descent united with riches."** Discuss and make notes on how the story of the De Lacey family illustrates this idea.

Chapters 15 and 16

The creature found books which became his daily reading. These were **The Sorrows of Werter**, **Plutarch's Lives** and **Paradise Lost**. From each of them he learned something different. He applied the sorrow and despair of Werter to his own miserable feelings as an outcast. He was uplifted by the lofty stories of heroes and rulers in Plutarch, learning of countries and kingdoms and the difference between the rule of a wise king and a despot. It was with two characters, Adam and Satan, in *Paradise Lost* with whom he most associated himself. Like Adam he had a creator, but unlike Adam he was not beautiful and protected, but hideous and abandoned. Like Satan he was cast out of Paradise, but unlike the fallen angel he had no companions to share his miserable exile.

The creature also found papers in the coat he had taken after his 'birth'. Now he could read them, he found an account of Frankenstein's work in making him and was angry at Victor's behaviour in first creating and then rejecting him.

The creature wanted to make himself known to the De Lacey family, trusting in their goodness and compassion to be accepted. When the blind old man was at home on his own, the creature spoke to him and told him of his sad situation. The old man was kind and accepted the creature he could not see. However, when Felix and the women saw him, Agatha fainted and Safie fled, while Felix tore the creature away from the old man and beat him with a stick. The creature did not retaliate but ran away instead.

The creature told how he hid in the woods while rage and despair filled his heart. Later he decided he had approached the family in the wrong way and would try to repair the damage. When he returned to the cottage and found the family had gone – too afraid of him to stay there – he determined on revenge and burned the cottage down.

The creature set out to find the only person he had a right to ask for anything – his creator. He headed for Geneva, travelling through the night and resting by day for fear of being seen. The winter passed and early in spring he was travelling through woods during the day when a young girl passed him and fell into the river. The creature rescued her and was trying to revive her when a young man rushed out and grabbed the girl from him. When the creature followed, the youth shot him and left him in agony. The wound in his shoulder gradually healed, but the hurt inside him grew into hatred for the man who had made him and left him an outcast.

At last he arrived near Geneva and was in hiding when a little boy disturbed him. The terrified child said his father was Frankenstein. In a fit of vengeful rage the creature strangled him, taking the miniature of Victor's mother from him. Looking for shelter he found Justine sleeping in a barn and, knowing he could never have a relationship with such a woman, he framed her for the murder by placing the miniature in her pocket. He then went to the mountains until he could meet Victor.

He tells Victor that the only way he will leave him alone is if he creates a female companion for him.

- The creature's reading teaches him about different aspects of human life, society and emotions but also how much of an outcast he is from these.
- His discovery of his origin from Victor's papers connects him with *Paradise Lost* but is also a contrast in its unnatural creation.
- His rejection by the admired De Lacey family and his later wounding turn his feelings into rage and desire for revenge, which is shown in the murder of William and framing of Justine.

> **Key quotations**
>
> **I learned from your papers that you were my father, my creator; and to whom could I apply with more fitness than to him who had given me life?** *(Chapter 16)*

Activity 9

Imagine you are a reporter for a local newspaper and have heard of a 'monster' in the neighbourhood. Write an article for your paper including the following:

- an interview with members of the De Lacey family
- an interview with the young couple in the woods
- an editorial column giving an opinion about the 'monster' and what it is
- a headline and appropriate sub-headings.

Base your account on what the creature says but include the sort of exaggeration typical of a news article.

Paradise Lost a long poem by John Milton that tells the story of the creation and fall of Man and of Lucifer/Satan

Plutarch's Lives the history of men who founded ideal republics and societies, both virtuous and vicious

The Sorrows of Werter a story by Goethe in which Werter falls in love and, in despair, commits suicide

Chapters 17 and 18

At first Victor refuses the request, but the creature argues that he feels hatred because he is solitary and a companion will give him sympathy. Victor realizes he owes his creation some happiness but is torn between compassion and loathing.

The creature promises he and his companion will live in the wilderness of South America and never trouble Victor again. However, if his one demand is refused, he will destroy Victor. At last Victor agrees and the creature leaves him, promising to watch the progress of his work.

Victor returns to Geneva depressed and ill, and his father is worried about him. He asks Victor if his low spirits are because of his engagement to Elizabeth and whether his affections have changed. Victor is adamant about his love for Elizabeth but tells his father he must travel to England. His true reason is to consult natural philosophers who have made discoveries that will help in his creation of the creature's mate. His father arranges for Henry Clerval to accompany him. Victor is anxious for his family but reasons that the creature will follow him to England to keep an eye on his progress. He and Clerval spend some happy days travelling down the River Rhine and arrive in London.

- The creature is shown to be eloquent and persuasive. His education has helped in this.
- Victor feels guilt and some compassion, which leads to his promise to create a mate for the creature.
- This means deferring his marriage to Elizabeth until the promise is fulfilled; something that has consequences later.

Key quotations

His words had a strange effect upon me. I compassionated him, and sometimes felt a wish to console him; but when I looked upon him, when I saw the filthy mass that moved and talked, my heart sickened, and my feelings were altered to those of horror and hatred. *(Chapter 17)*

Activity 10

With a partner, take turns to interview each other in the role of Victor and the creature. Write three or four open questions based on the novel to ask each other in role. Answer from the conversation in the novel but in your own words.

Chapters 19 and 20

Victor and Henry spend time in London and Victor learns what he needs to know. They then receive an invitation to travel to Scotland, which Victor sees as an opportunity to complete his work in isolation. After travelling to Oxford, they proceed to the Lake District, which they admire, and then to Edinburgh and Perth. Here Victor parts from Clerval, saying he must have solitude, and he goes to the Orkneys. In this barren place he continues his work, motivated by terror for his family and friends, and with horror at what he must do. He looks forward to completing the work with both hope and a presentiment of evil.

As Victor completes his female creature, he questions the promise he made. She has not made the same promise as the male creature and might be capable of worse acts. Even more frightful, there could be children and a whole race of malignant creatures that would destroy mankind. As he thinks, Victor sees the creature at the window and he destroys the female he has been creating.

The creature later visits him and, seeing Victor will not change his mind, threatens to make him repent his decision. He quits the hovel, promising to be with Victor on his wedding night. Victor cleans the laboratory and takes the pieces he has torn apart in a boat to get rid of them. After throwing

The creature attacks Frankenstein, his creator, in the 1994 film *Mary Shelley's Frankenstein*

the basket of pieces into the sea, he falls asleep and wakes to find he has drifted far from the Orkneys. After many hours he arrives in a town in Ireland, where he is arrested for the murder of a stranger found near the shore.

- Victor's apparent need to consult English scientists gives him a reason to put off his wedding and for the reader to observe his closeness to Clerval.

- As he progresses with making the female creature in the wilds of Orkney, Victor has time to consider the possible outcome.

- His destruction of the creature's mate sets in motion the final train of events that lead to his own death.

Key quotations

"It is well. I go; but remember, I shall be with you on your wedding-night." *(Chapter 20)*

Activity 11

What do the following quotations from Chapter 20 suggest about Victor's feelings? Make a note of your answers.

- **Had I right, for my own benefit, to inflict this curse upon everlasting generations?**

- **I shuddered to think who might be the next victim sacrificed to his insatiate revenge.**

- **The remains of the half-finished creature, whom I had destroyed, lay scattered on the floor, and I almost felt as if I had mangled the flesh of a living human being.**

- **I felt as if I was about the commission of a dreadful crime, and avoided with shuddering anxiety any encounter with my fellow-creatures.**

Chapters 21 and 22

Victor discovers that the murdered stranger is Henry Clerval and is so distraught he becomes ill. He is nursed in prison. The magistrate finds a letter from Victor's father in the son's pocket and sends for him. Victor's father tells him his family are well and stays with him until the trial. Victor is acquitted as it is proved that he was on Orkney when the murder took place. He is despairing and tries to commit suicide but is restrained by his father, who takes him away from Ireland.

In Paris, where they break their journey, Victor declines any society and accuses himself of murdering William, Justine and Henry. He receives a letter from Elizabeth, asking if his melancholy is due to doubts about their marriage and assuring him of her love. Victor is sure that the creature will kill him on his wedding night but he writes to Elizabeth that she is his only happiness but that he has a dreadful secret which he will tell her after their wedding.

As the date draws closer, he has to hide his feelings and pretend to be a happy bridegroom. He carries pistols and a knife wherever he goes as protection and this reassures him. After the marriage ceremony, Victor and Elizabeth take a boat to Evian on the first stage of their honeymoon to Como.

- The murder of Clerval is the creature's immediate response to Victor's broken promise and once again Frankenstein's illness is a response to guilt.

- Victor's father is seen here as his rescuer and protector, saving him from imprisonment and later from suicide.

- Victor is so convinced that his wedding night is his own death sentence that he doesn't see any other possibility.

Key quotations

Great God! If for one instant I had thought what might be the hellish intention of my fiendish adversary, I would rather have banished myself for ever from my native country, and wandered a friendless outcast over the earth, than have consented to this miserable marriage. *(Chapter 22)*

Activity 12

Discuss or consider the following questions, making notes of your ideas.

- What is the difference between Victor's treatment after his arrest and that of Justine Moritz?

- What role does Victor's father play in each case?

- Why do you think Mary Shelley includes two similar arrests of innocents for murder but gives them such different outcomes?

Chapters 23 and 24

Victor and Elizabeth reach an inn on the lake and Victor's fears grow as the night comes down. Elizabeth is worried for him, but he tells her that after this night all will be safe. Not wanting her to see his struggle with the creature, he suggests she goes to bed. He searches all the rooms but finds no signs of the creature until he hears a scream from the bedroom. Victor realizes the creature's true intention and rushes into the room to find Elizabeth dead on the bed. He faints away and when he comes round he rushes to take his wife in his arms and sees the creature jeering at him from the window. Pulling out a pistol he fires, but misses and the creature runs into the lake. A search party goes after the creature but finds nothing.

Victor then thinks his father and brother must be in danger and he hurries back to Geneva to find them both alive. His father is bowed down by Elizabeth's death and dies in Victor's arms a few days later.

Victor has no recollection of the time following his father's death but comes back to his senses to find himself confined as a madman. Driven by hatred, he goes to the magistrate and recites his story, demanding that the creature be pursued and arrested. The magistrate points out the difficulties of following such a monster. Victor is angry at the lack of help and rushes from the house.

Victor dedicates the rest of his life to a 'search and destroy' mission against the creature, who waylays him at the tomb of his family and challenges him to follow. The creature leads him across the countries of Europe and beyond, giving him little rest or repose. His only consolation is in his sleep when he dreams he is with his family and friends. The creature keeps him alive by providing food and water in desperate times and leaving jeering messages where Victor will see them.

At last, the creature heads for the Arctic wastes and Victor buys a sled and dog team and follows. He gains on the creature but when it seems he will catch up, the frozen sea cracks apart and he is left on an ice raft. He then sees Walton's ship and allows himself to be rescued when he finds it is going north.

- Victor's blindness to the creature's real intention leads to Elizabeth's death and, indirectly, to his father's.
- Yet again, guilt shows itself in illness, both physical and mental.
- Victor becomes a friendless outcast, wandering the earth after the creature he now resembles.

Key quotations

And now my wanderings began, which are to cease but with life. *(Chapter 24)*

Activity 13

Create a map showing the journey Victor makes in pursuit of the creature. You should include quotations at appropriate points showing events and feelings.

Letter 4 continued

After Frankenstein has finished his story he shows Walton letters from Felix and Safie which, along with the appearance of the creature on the ice, convince him the tale is true. When Walton tries to get the detail of the creature's creation from him, Frankenstein refuses point blank to disclose knowledge that would lead to misery. Frankenstein tells Walton he had been born to do great things, but has ended wretched and despairing, and warns him against doing the same. He asks that if he should die Walton should finish the task of destroying the creature. Walton wonders if he will ever escape from the walls of ice that threaten to crush the ship. His crew revolt and make him promise that if they are freed he will sail south and not continue his journey to the pole. Frankenstein tries to make them regain pride in their quest but the men insist they will return home.

A week later the ice splits and, as they begin their journey south, Frankenstein dies. As he is writing his journal that night, Walton hears noises from Victor's cabin and finds the creature lamenting his dead creator. He tells Walton that his revenge has given him extreme misery and remorse. At first he had looked for virtue and affection until he learned otherwise from people's behaviour towards him. Now he is miserable and degraded and fit only for self-destruction. He tells Walton he will go to the North Pole, build a funeral pyre and throw himself on it, thus ending his misery and any threat to humans. He springs from the cabin window onto his ice raft and is carried away into the darkness.

- Robert Walton writes to his sister and tells of Frankenstein's death.
- Victor's warning to Walton against proud ambition now bears fruit and Walton listens to his crew.
- Walton's encounter with the creature ties up the final loose ends of the story as we know he will destroy himself.

Key quotations

Fear not that I shall be the instrument of future mischief. My work is nearly complete. Neither yours nor any man's death is needed to consummate the series of my being, and accomplish that which must be done; but it requires my own. *(Chapter 24)*

Activity 14

Find quotations from the creature's speeches to Walton that support the following statements:

- He feels affection and grief for Victor.
- He feels guilt and remorse for his actions.
- His actions were prompted by revenge.
- He once wanted only to be loved and virtuous.
- He suffered injustice from Victor.

Structure

The structure of the novel follows the classic three-act pattern.

The first Act of the novel tells of Walton's voyage and his rescue of Victor Frankenstein. From Frankenstein he hears the story of his childhood and the education that inspired him to become a scientist. Victor is prompted to tell his story because he recognizes the fatal ambition in Robert Walton that caused his own downfall: **"Unhappy man! Do you share my madness? Have you drank also of the intoxicating draught? Hear me, – let me reveal my tale, and you will dash the cup from your lips!'"** *(Letter 4)* This part ends with his creation and abandonment of the creature. This is the **inciting incident**.

inciting incident the event that leads to everything else in the story

The second Act is concerned with the murder of William and Justine's execution. It includes the creature's story and Victor's promise to provide the creature with a mate. The making and then destruction of the creature's mate leads to a spate of revenge killings culminating in the murder of Elizabeth and the subsequent death of

Victor's father: "I may die; but first you, my tyrant and tormentor, shall curse the sun that gazes on your misery." *(Chapter 20)* This is the **climax**.

The third Act follows Frankenstein's search for the creature and his death on Walton's ship. It takes in Walton's decision to return home. The end comes when the creature announces its own death and is taken out of sight. "I shall die, and what I now feel be no longer felt." *(Chapter 24)* This is the **resolution**.

> **climax** the event to which everything has been building
>
> **resolution** the way everything works out

Activity 15

1. Make a diagram of the three-act structure of *Frankenstein*, showing how all the important events fit into this pattern.

2. Discuss the ending and how satisfactory or otherwise you consider it.

Viewpoint

The story of *Frankenstein* is told in multiple narratives:

- Walton's letters to his sister form the enclosing or outer narrative.
- Inside this is Victor's story of his creation of the creature and subsequent disasters.
- Within this again is the creature's story of its development, education and exclusion, which is the heart of the novel.

These layers of narrative are all linked, partly because of the similarities between the characters (see the sections on Characters and Themes), and, in some cases, parallel to them. Within these layers are other stories, letters and journals. This use of stories-within-stories has different effects:

- It makes Victor's incredible story seem more believable because he is telling it to Walton, who is writing it down for his sister.
- The reader can make their own judgment about the characters from hearing the different stories.
- It distances the reader from the events in the tales, partly because the narrators sometimes address their audience directly. This also gives the story authenticity.
- It places the creature's story at the heart of the novel, just as his creation is at the heart of all the main events.

The three male narrators are linked, either directly or indirectly. Walton shares Frankenstein's culture and desire to extend the boundaries of knowledge, as well as his egotism. Victor and the creature are linked closely as 'father/creator' and 'child/creation'. They come together finally on Walton's ship where they both meet death.

Mary Shelley has chosen not to use an **omniscient narrator**, but tells the story from the viewpoints of the three main characters, who act as narrators. The reader does not get a single overall point of view or opinion, which means they must rely on their own judgment to decide on the rights or wrongs of the characters' behaviour. The reader must be like a detective, looking for clues that suggest how far a character may be trusted. The main clues they have are in the matching of the characters' words and actions. The reader also needs to be aware of the reactions of others to these words and actions, both explicit and implicit.

> **Key quotations**
>
> ... **I own to you that the letters of Felix and Safie, which he showed me, and the apparition of the monster seen from our ship, brought to me a greater conviction of the truth of his narrative than his asseverations, however earnest and connected.** (*Chapter 24*)

omniscient narrator a storyteller who knows what all the characters are doing, saying and thinking

Activity 16

Re-read the paragraph towards the end of Chapter 7 that begins '**This speech calmed me.**' and ends '**... which I had let loose upon the world?**'

a) Rewrite this paragraph in the manner of an omniscient narrator who has their own opinion of the events.

b) Compare your paragraph with the original and note the differences.

c) Discuss your findings with other students, exchanging notes and ideas.

Timescale

The main events of the story take place over about ten years. They include references and flashbacks to Victor's childhood, which give the reader a picture of his family life and formative influences. Victor tells his tale to Walton within a much briefer time span of a few months. This gives the novel its clarity and organization.

Writing about plot and structure

Upgrade

You need to know the novel very thoroughly. Although you may not be questioned directly on its plot, you need to show that you understand all the key events and why they happen. This doesn't mean you should retell the story, but you should be able to select events that are relevant to the question.

When writing about the structure of the novel and its viewpoint, you should include the idea of multiple narratives and give reasons why the author has chosen to use this method of telling the story.

Biography of Mary Wollstonecraft Shelley

Mary Wollstonecraft Shelley, 1797–1851

- She was born in 1797 in London to the radical thinker and writer, William Godwin and Mary Wollstonecraft, author of *A Vindication of the Rights of Women*. Her mother died soon after Mary's birth. Mary often visited her grave with her father. Attitudes to women are one of the motifs of *Frankenstein*, although Mary Shelley's treatment is subtle.

- She grew up in a household of revolutionary ideas where writers like Samuel Taylor Coleridge, William Blake and William Wordsworth, as well as thinkers such as Humphrey Davy and radical politicians like Horne Tooke, were visitors. Their ideas affected her own outlook on life. The story of *Frankenstein* hinges on the nature of society and the pursuit of knowledge.

- Mary Shelley was not formally educated, however she had access to her father's well-stocked library and educated herself in philosophy, science and politics as well as poetry and **gothic** novels. This was all knowledge she brought to the writing of *Frankenstein*.

- At 16, Mary ran away with Percy Shelley, one of the Romantic poets and a revolutionary who was married at the time and one of her father's protégés. She became Mary Shelley after his wife committed suicide. They had four children. The first child, born in 1815, lived only 11 days and Mary dreamed that it had come to life again after being warmed by the fire. This may have affected the way ideas of birth, death and parenting are treated in *Frankenstein*.

- Percy and Mary travelled to Switzerland in 1816, staying at Lake Geneva next to Lord Byron and joining his dinner parties at the Villa Diodati. The weather was poor and the party occupied themselves writing ghost stories. It was from this impetus that *Frankenstein* was written. While they were away, Mary Shelley's half-sister committed suicide, as did Percy Shelley's wife Harriet. There may be echoes of these tragedies in the theme of life and death within the novel.

- The Shelleys remained in Italy, travelling around until, in 1822, Percy Shelley was drowned off the coast of Italy. Mary and her surviving child returned to England soon after. She continued writing, publishing articles, stories and novels and editing her husband's last poems. She died in 1851 at the age of 53. Her legacy is a novel that continues to stir the imagination of readers and directors.

gothic a literary genre that contains wild and picturesque scenery, melodramatic events which may be supernatural and an atmosphere of dread and horror

Tips for assessment

You should only make reference to the author's life if it is relevant to something in the text or helps to explain her intentions in writing *Frankenstein*.

The writing of *Frankenstein*

This is a story in itself, told in the Preface to the 1831 edition by the author. The Shelleys spent time with Lord Byron on Lake Geneva and the weather was so bad that they stayed indoors reading gothic stories. As a result, a competition was proposed to write a ghost story. *Frankenstein* was Mary Shelley's contribution.

Activity 1

Read the Introduction to the novel, which explains how it came to be written.

a) Select three events that you think contributed to the story.

b) Find an appropriate quotation for each, to support your choice.

c) Write a paragraph showing how these real events affected the finished novel.

The overthrow of traditional order during the French Revolution

Historical setting

At the time Mary Shelley was writing *Frankenstein* – during the reign of George III and the Regency of the future George IV – the American War of Independence and the French Revolution were still within memory and they helped to fuel the Radical Movement in Britain and elsewhere. The French Revolution began with the storming of the notorious prison of the Bastille in Paris, in 1789. It was driven by the grievances of people whose suffering was ignored by the rulers. There followed a period of lawlessness with people suspected of belonging to the ruling class being strung from lampposts. The French royal family and members of their court were sent to the guillotine and a Republic was declared. At first the British radicals rejoiced and hoped for a similar overthrow of repressive British rule, but the bloodshed became so excessive that many turned against French ideas.

Mary's parents were radical activists and writers, and so were many of their guests, including Percy Shelley. The Radicals were influenced by the writings of Thomas Paine (*The Rights of Man*), who promoted the idea that everyone should have a say in how they were governed. This was a revolutionary stance as far as the king and Parliament were concerned, and the Radicals were arrested for treason. William Godwin saw the necessity for people to work together for social good, while Mary Wollstonecraft wrote of the need to include women in social and political life. All these views inevitably helped to form Mary's own. In *Frankenstein* Victor creates new life without a woman, which goes against the natural order and threatens society.

Power in Britain was firmly in the hands of the monarchy and the **aristocracy**, supported by the **landed gentry**, who formed the Houses of Parliament. Very few people had a vote at this time unless they were already wealthy. The ruling class, having witnessed events in France, were fearful of the effects of a possible revolution to create a republic in Britain. They used repressive laws carried out by the army to enforce their decrees. The fate of the De Lacey family shows what happened to those who questioned authority, whether in France or England. The creature may represent the revolutionaries, who were driven to revolt by their harsh treatment and the rejection of their pleas for food and employment.

In a political sense, the novel can be read as a warning of the dangers of letting loose the monster of **anarchy** and revolution within society or as a warning to rulers about their treatment of the poor and the results that may occur.

Key quotations

I learned that the possessions most esteemed by your fellow-creatures were, high and unsullied descent united with riches. A man might be respected with only one of these advantages; but, without either, he was considered, except in very rare circumstances, as a vagabond and slave, doomed to waste his powers for the profits of the chosen few! *(Chapter 13)*

Activity 2

a) Research the following topics:

- the French Revolution
- the Radical Movement in England, 1780–1830
- the place of women in Regency England
- the role of Parliament in Regency England.

b) Write a brief summary of your findings in not more than 200 words.

c) Compare your findings with other students.

Social and cultural context

In the mid-18th century, Britain was a mainly rural and agricultural economy. Products were made by craftsmen such as weavers using hand looms, carpenters making individual items of furniture or stonemasons building houses and bridges. The **Industrial Revolution** demonstrated progress in science and technology as new methods of mining coal enabled more powerful steam engines to increase production in factories, and improved techniques for making iron and steel led to better structures and machines.

However, the working conditions for those (including children) who mined the coal and produced the iron were harsh, dangerous and poorly paid. This was also the case in many factories where people worked 12–14 hours a day in conditions where they were breathing in minute fibres and in danger from unguarded machines. If workers became ill, they were sacked without pay and faced starvation.

The transport revolution which saw the building of canals to link Britain's waterways, led to more rapid movement of coal, and other products, to the towns where it powered the machines in factories.

At the same time, the enclosure of **common land** by gentlemen farmers and the development of agricultural machinery led to an increase in unemployment and poverty among rural labourers – something that Wordsworth exposed in his poetry. Some people, known as Luddites, were desperate enough to break the factory machines that were taking away their livelihoods. If caught, they would be executed.

The poverty the creature observes while in hiding is set in France but was just as real in Britain. People were driven to towns in search of employment in the new factories, which led to overcrowded slums and the spread of disease. The scarlet fever that killed Frankenstein's mother was only one of many deadly illnesses that carried people off before their time. The monster here can be viewed as industrialization, which equates people to machines rather than craftsmen and takes away individuality, just as Victor's creation is beyond his control and threatens him.

anarchy a state without rulers where every individual has complete freedom; a state of lawlessness and disorder without rulers or laws

aristocracy those with titles and wealth who owned large estates and stately homes, including members of the royal family

common land green spaces that were held in common by villagers who were entitled to graze their animals on them for free

Industrial Revolution the period when goods started to be made by machines in factories. It was brought about by the use of coal instead of wood, allowing steam engines to be used and iron to be processed more efficiently

landed gentry the social level just below the aristocracy, which owned local manor houses and smaller estates, and sometimes mixed with the aristocracy

Dangerous and dehumanizing conditions in an iron mill in 1875

> **Key quotations**
>
> … it was poverty; and they suffered that evil in a very distressing degree. Their nourishment consisted entirely of the vegetables of their garden, and the milk of one cow, which gave very little during the winter, when its masters could scarcely procure food to support it. *(Chapter 12)*

The Age of Enlightenment

At a time when rational thought and scientific discovery were valued, many educated people discussed the place of science and religion in society. The ideas of Jean Jacques Rousseau were popular, which envisaged the child as an innocent 'blank slate' until corrupted by society. This idea is seen in the creature's question, "**… tell me why I should pity man more than he pities me?**" *(Chapter 17)* The possibility of exploring the ways of Nature and harnessing her power is shown in the striking of the oak tree by lightning. Galvanism demonstrated that dead animals being could apparently be 'brought to life' by the use of electric currents.

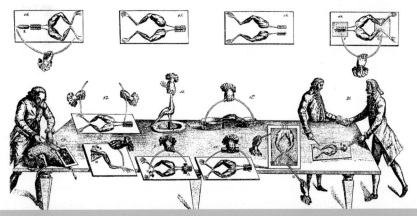

Luigi Galvani's work on frogs in 1780 represented the first experiments into the field of Bioelectricity, which still studies the electrical patterns of the nervous system

Mary Shelley used these ideas in her creation of the creature. Victor's growth as a scientist takes him from medieval alchemy, through the study of Mathematics to Natural Philosophy – or the sciences, as we would know them. It also contains ideas gleaned from contemporary science including Humphry Davy's book *Elements of Chemical Philosophy*, in which he wrote that 'science has... bestowed upon man powers which may be called creative; which have enabled him to change and modify the beings around him...'.

The apparently fine line between life and death was a topic that fascinated doctors and scientists. In the novel, fainting and illness are described in terms of death, **'But I was not the witness of his grief; for I was lifeless, and did not recover my senses for a long, long time.'** *(Chapter 5)* Death itself was not always easy to decide with certainty and gave rise to horror stories of premature burials or near escapes.

Key quotations

After days and nights of incredible labour and fatigue, I succeeded in discovering the cause of generation and life; nay, more, I became myself capable of bestowing animation upon lifeless matter. *(Chapter 4)*

Activity 3

Briefly research the following people:

- Erasmus Darwin
- Humphrey Davy
- Jean Jacques Rousseau
- Luigi Galvani.

Put your results together as the basis for an article for a student magazine on Mary Shelley's use of science in *Frankenstein*. It should include quotations from the novel where appropriate and not exceed 200 words in total.

Literary context

The Romantic Movement

Both Percy Shelley and Lord Byron were Romantic poets, as was William Blake, who frequented the Godwin house and Samuel Taylor Coleridge whose *The Rime of the Ancient Mariner* inspired Mary Shelley as a child. Romanticism was a movement that stressed the importance of feelings and emotions, especially in relation to Nature and the individual's relationship with it. It is notable that both Frankenstein and the creature are moved by Nature and scenery.

Many Romantic works had gothic themes and subjects, including Coleridge's *Ancient Mariner*, which so appeals to Walton. The Romantic writers were radical in their politics, portraying the misery of the poor and repression by the government as in Percy Shelley's poem 'Masque of Anarchy' or William Blake's 'London'. The fact that *Frankenstein* was inspired by a dream would also place it in the Romantic genre, since dreams were one of the manifestations of feelings and consciousness considered important. Victor's dream just after he has created the creature is also significant. The horrors of graveyards and the supernatural – as the creature's strength and endurance seem to be – could be found in the gothic novels of the time such as Walpole's *The Castle of Otranto*.

Milton and *Paradise Lost*

The idea of 'the modern Prometheus' is associated with the notion of Satan and Adam in *Paradise Lost*. Prometheus was cast out of heaven in Greek mythology for daring to steal fire from the gods and give it to humans. This is a parallel for Frankenstein's search for knowledge with which he hopes to benefit his fellows. He is punished for his presumption, just as Prometheus was punished for his. The creature sees himself both as Satan – cast down to hell by his creator for wanting to equal God – and Adam, newly created but driven from Paradise because he seeks knowledge. Mary Shelley knew Milton's epic poem well and she uses it to represent the struggle between good and evil that underpins the novel.

The Rime of the Ancient Mariner

Coleridge's poem apparently inspired Robert Walton to undertake his voyage to the Arctic. It tells the story of a mariner who is under a curse and compelled to tell his story to someone who has no choice but to listen (much as Walton listens to Frankenstein and Frankenstein to the creature). The Mariner was on a ship that sailed to 'the land of ice and snow' but, on a whim, he shot an albatross that had befriended the sailors. This caused the ship to be becalmed in the Sargasso Sea, where all the crew died around him. His crime against Nature echoes that of Victor Frankenstein, while the setting is similar to the plain of ice that traps Walton's ship.

> **Key quotations**
>
> I am going to unexplored regions, to 'the land of mist and snow;' but I shall kill no albatross, therefore do not be alarmed for my safety, or if I should come back to you as worn and woeful as the 'Ancient Mariner?' (*Letter 2*)
>
> But 'Paradise Lost' excited different and far deeper emotions. … It moved every feeling of wonder and awe that the picture of an omnipotent God warring with his creatures was capable of exciting. (*Chapter 15*)

Activity 4

Read the quotations below from some of the writers mentioned above. Consider how these quotations could be relevant to the events or background of the novel.

> Is this a holy thing to see
> In a rich and fruitful land, –
> Babes reduced to misery,
> Fed with cold and usurous hand?
> (From *Songs of Innocence and Experience* by William Blake)

> The ice was here, the ice was there,
> The ice was all around:
> It cracked and growled, and roared and howled,
> Like noises in a swound!
> (From *The Rime of the Ancient Mariner* by Samuel Taylor Coleridge)

> God made thee of choice his own, and of his own
> To serve him, thy reward was of his grace,
> Thy punishment then justly is at his Will.
> (From *Paradise Lost* by John Milton, referring to Adam and Eve being evicted from Paradise)

> My happy father died
> When sad distress reduced the childrens' meal:
> Thrice happy! that from him the grave did hide
> The empty loom, cold hearth, and silent wheel,
> And tears that flowed for ills which patience could not heal.
> (From *The Female Vagrant* by William Wordsworth)

Critical reaction

The novel was originally published anonymously as it was thought that female authorship might have spoiled its chances of publication. It was much later that Mary Shelley published it under her own name. The reaction of one reviewer shows why. *The British Critic* attacked the novel's flaws as the fault of the author:

> The writer of it is, we understand, a female; this is an aggravation of that which is the prevailing fault of the novel; but if our authoress can forget the gentleness of her sex, it is no reason why we should; and we shall therefore dismiss the novel without further comment.

This is part of Sir Walter Scott's review of *Frankenstein* for *Blackwood's Magazine*, after the novel's original publication in 1818:

> It is no slight merit in our eyes, that the tale, though wild in incident, is written in plain and forcible English, without exhibiting that mixture of **hyperbolical Germanisms** with which tales of wonder are usually told, as if it were necessary that the language should be as extravagant as the fiction. The ideas of the author are always clearly as well as forcibly expressed; and his descriptions of landscape have in them the choice requisites of truth, freshness, precision, and beauty.

Other reviewers were unkind about the novel but this may have been due to its dedication to William Godwin, whose radical opinions were disapproved of by many. The public generally enjoyed the novel as another work from the gothic horror genre which was popular at the time.

Since the mid-20th century the novel has been praised for its moral and aesthetic relevance and has been cited as the first science fiction novel. The author Stephen King sees it as a 'Shakespearian tragedy', saying, 'its classical unity is broken only by the author's uncertainty as to where the fatal flaw lies – is it in Victor's **hubris** (usurping a power that belongs only to God) or in his failure to take responsibility for his creation after endowing it with the life-spark?'

Soon after its publication, the novel was dramatized as a stage play. It was made into a film as early as 1910, and since then there have been numerous other films and stage versions.

hubris a term from Greek drama meaning extreme pride and arrogance that leads to a character's downfall

hyperbolical Germanisms Scott seems to mean the more overblown emotional style of writers such as Schiller and Goethe

Activity 5

Although many films have been made of *Frankenstein*, none of them has truly followed the story written in Mary Shelley's book. Imagine a film has now been made that stays faithful to the original story.

a) Write the following:

- a synopsis of the film

- a catchphrase to persuade people to see it

- two scenes from the film featuring important moments. Set these out as a screenplay, including directions for the background and action, dialogue and some indication of camera angles. You could construct this as a storyboard if you wish.

b) Compare your work with others and discuss reasons for your choices.

Writing about context

Upgrade

This Context section is to help you understand the novel and Mary Shelley's reasons for writing it. You will not be expected to include contextual material in your answer unless it is relevant to the point you are making. It is also important to remember that you should not include much contextual information in your responses unless that is one of the assessment criteria for your exam board.

If you need to show you have understood the author's intentions, only a brief reference is required. For example, Mary Shelley's dream about a creature being made and coming to life is reproduced almost exactly in the account of Frankenstein's creation of his creature.

Main characters

Victor Frankenstein

He is the main **protagonist** of the novel and gives the novel its title. When the reader first meets Victor, he is being rescued by Robert Walton from the Arctic ice. Walton thinks he has found a kindred spirit and confides his ambitions to Frankenstein. This provides the stimulus for Victor to tell his story, which occupies most of the novel.

Mary Shelley shows Victor's childhood as being happy and carefree. The author provides no motive in Victor's upbringing that would give him an excuse for turning against God and Nature or cutting himself off from society. The only explanation he gives is that '**The world was to me a secret which I desired to divine. Curiosity, earnest research to learn the hidden laws of nature, gladness akin to rapture, as they were unfolded to me, are among the earliest sensations I can remember.**' *(Chapter 2)* At one point he appears to blame his father for not explaining why the works of Cornelius Agrippa were unworthy of study which, he says, might have prevented his later '**fatal impulse**' *(Chapter 2)*. In spite of being dazzled by the effects of lightning and galvanism to the point of abandoning Natural History for Mathematics, Frankenstein insists that '**Destiny was too potent, and her immutable laws had decreed my utter and terrible destruction.**' *(Chapter 2)* Victor is suggesting that his downfall was all the fault of fate and little to do with his own free will.

In writing Victor's account in the first person, the author allows us to see the workings of his mind and personality. His obsessive approach to his studies makes him seem a little mad, especially as he ignores his family, including his fiancée Elizabeth, in order to carry on his investigations beyond the end of his university course. He is determined to discover the principles of life and appears to be self-sufficient, without the need for human company or anything but his scientific experiments. '**Winter, spring, and summer passed away during my labours; but I did not watch the blossom or the expanding leaves – sights which before always yielded me supreme delight – so deeply was I engrossed in my occupation.**' *(Chapter 4)* When he finally succeeds in giving life to his human creature he is immediately filled with horror and disgust at its appearance and abandons it.

Frankenstein is arrogant as well as selfish. He feels no doubt either about his ability to create a human being or the morality of doing so: '… **I was surprised, that among so many men of genius who had directed their enquiries towards the same science, that I alone should have been reserved to discover so astonishing a secret**' *(Chapter 4)*. He appears to have no consideration at all for the likely feelings of the being he creates. He thinks of the creature solely in terms of a scientific experiment that will bring him glory and gratitude. Not content with making a new human being, he goes further: '**A new species would bless me as its creator and source; many happy and excellent natures would owe their being to me.**

No father could claim the gratitude of his child so completely as I should deserve theirs.' *(Chapter 4)* Accordingly he makes his creature of **'gigantic stature'**, not out of necessity but because **'the minuteness of the parts formed a great hindrance to my speed'** *(Chapter 4)*. Having abandoned his creature to the world because of his hideous appearance, Victor then blames it entirely for the evil deeds it commits due to his rejection.

Kenneth Branagh portrays Victor's obsessive nature in the 1994 film *Mary Shelley's Frankenstein*

When Victor finally returns home, six years after leaving for Ingolstadt, it is as a result of William's murder, which a meeting with the creature convinces him was his doing. Only then does Victor think **'Alas! I had turned loose into the world a depraved wretch, whose delight was in carnage and misery; had he not murdered my brother?'** *(Chapter 7)* He never once considers that doing his duty to the creature as the one who made him might have prevented this outcome. It is not until the creature forces him to listen to his story that Frankenstein feels a twinge of concern about what he owes him: **'His tale, and the feelings he now expressed, proved him to be a creature of fine sensations, and did I not, as his maker, owe him all the portion of happiness that it was in my power to bestow?'** *(Chapter 17)*

> **immutable** unable to be changed
>
> **protagonist** the main character in a novel

It is not until he is on the point of completing the promised female that Victor begins to outline the arguments he should have debated before creating his creature in the first place: 'Had I right, for my own benefit, to inflict this curse upon everlasting generations? I had before been moved by the sophisms of the being I had created; I had been struck senseless by his fiendish threats: but now, for the first time, the wickedness of my promise burst upon me; I shuddered to think that future ages might curse me as their pest, whose selfishness had not hesitated to buy its own peace at the price, perhaps, of the existence of the whole human race.' *(Chapter 20)* It is noticeable that Victor's main argument here concerns his own reputation. Throughout his story he tells nobody what he has done. He allows Justine to be hanged for William's murder when he knows who is responsible: 'The poor victim, who on the morrow was to pass the awful boundary between life and death, felt not as I did, such deep and bitter agony.' *(Chapter 8)* He keeps his secret from Clerval, denying him the knowledge that his life could be in danger. He even allows Elizabeth to be murdered rather than tell her what danger she could be in. It seems incredible that he imagines the creature's promise to be with him on his wedding night as a threat only to himself. Mary Shelley is making use of **dramatic irony** here, since the reader will almost certainly have grasped the creature's real meaning straight after Victor destroys his mate.

Victor's love for his mother is deep and it is her death that sets him on the path to discovering the secret of restoring life. For all his protestations of love for Elizabeth, he leaves her for university and stays away for six years. Despite the thought that she could be in danger, he leaves again for England in order to make a mate for the creature, saying, 'Alas! to me the idea of an immediate union with my Elizabeth was one of horror and dismay.' *(Chapter 18)* This reaction hardly suggests the strong desire of a lover. When he does finally marry her, he sends Elizabeth to bed on her own while he awaits the creature.

Modern commentators have noted his apparent distaste for sexuality, considering that he wants to create new life by bypassing the sexual act. The being that he creates, intending it to be beautiful, is a male, while the incomplete creature he destroys is a female, saying that she might be worse than a male and able to reproduce. The being he loves most throughout the novel is Henry Clerval. He seems far more grief-stricken when Clerval is murdered than when Elizabeth is killed. In his dream after the creature's creation, Elizabeth turns into his mother's decaying corpse.

> **dramatic irony** the situation where the audience knows something that the characters don't

It is the death of his father that sends Victor into true madness and he spends some time locked in an asylum. '**What then became of me? I know not; I lost sensation, and chains and darkness were the only objects that pressed upon me.**' *(Chapter 23)* He then resolves to spend the rest of his life on a mission to destroy the creature, making a melodramatic oath of vengeance. He follows the creature across the continent to the Arctic wastes where he finally dies on Walton's ship after telling his story for posterity.

Right to the end he shows no genuine remorse for his attempt to usurp the powers of God and Nature for he tells Walton, "**During these last days I have been occupied in examining my past conduct; nor do I find it blamable.**" *(Chapter 24)* This appears an astonishing conclusion, given what his folly has caused.

> **Key quotations**
>
> **Pursuing these reflections, I thought, that if I could bestow animation upon lifeless matter, I might in process of time (although I now found it impossible) renew life where death had apparently devoted the body to corruption.** *(Chapter 4)*

Activity 1

In a group of six, each take one of the following roles:

- the creature
- Elizabeth Lavenza
- Justine Moritz
- Henry Clerval
- Alphonse Frankenstein
- Victor Frankenstein.

a) Each character, except Victor, should write about how Victor's own attitude and actions affected their life. Victor should write a defence of his attitude and actions. Try not to exceed 200 words. Base your writing on the novel and include quotations to support what you say.

b) Stage a hearing, in which each character makes their accusation, including their own feelings. Finally Victor should make his defence against each accusation.

The creature

One of the saddest things about the creature is that he has no name and therefore his only identity is 'the monster' or 'the creature' or the names that Victor calls him.

Victor describes him as he comes to life: **'His limbs were in proportion, and I had selected his features as beautiful. Beautiful! – Great God! His yellow skin scarcely covered the work of muscles and arteries beneath; his hair was of a lustrous black, and flowing; his teeth of a pearly whiteness; but these luxuriances only formed a more horrid contrast with his watery eyes, that seemed almost of the same colour as the dun white sockets in which they were set, his shrivelled complexion and straight black lips.'** *(Chapter 5)* Having woken from one dream, Victor later awakes from a nightmare to see the creature by his bed. The creature tries to speak to him and stretches out a hand with a grin, presumably in the hope of parental fondness. Instead of recognition he is once more abandoned.

Frankenstein's creature is forced to set out into the world on his own

The reader hears no more of the creature until he meets Victor on his return to Geneva and Victor realizes the creature has murdered William. After Justine's trial and execution, Victor meets the creature on Montanvert, a mountain near Mont Blanc, and we finally hear what happened to him. With the recital of the creature's story, Mary Shelley changes our sympathies because we see things from his point of view. Like any newborn he has to learn to distinguish between sensations but unlike most infants he has to clothe and feed himself and learn about the world through trial and error as the episode with the fire shows. The creature is puzzled and upset to find that people react to him with fear and aggression and he learns to hide away from humans.

When he finds shelter he discovers the De Lacey family and from them he learns how a loving family behaves. Their care for each other makes a deep impression on him. He admires their attractive appearance and is horrified when he sees his own reflection and realizes why people fear him. From them, he learns empathy: **'The gentle manners and beauty of the cottagers greatly endeared them to me: when they were unhappy, I felt depressed; when they rejoiced, I sympathised in their joys.'** *(Chapter 12)* This leads him to help them by doing chores such as chopping wood and clearing snow, and he dreams of making himself known to them.

From observing Felix and Safie, the creature learns about the nature of love between man and woman, and he learns the language as she does. His education is widened as he learns to read and he begins to reflect on the nature of the society he hears about. He wonders whether he is even human as he has seen none like himself. **'I was more agile than they, and could subsist upon coarser diet; I bore the extremes of heat and cold with less injury to my frame; my stature far exceeded theirs.'** *(Chapter 13)* He asks **'Was I then a monster, a blot upon the earth, from which all men fled, and whom all men disowned?'** *(Chapter 13)* It is this physical superiority that enables him to track Frankenstein and appear where Victor is least expecting him. This ability and his strength are what enables him to get the upper hand.

When the creature reads *Paradise Lost* he is uncertain whether to identify with Adam or Satan: **'Like Adam, I was apparently united by no link to any other being in existence; … Many times I considered Satan as the fitter emblem of my condition; for often, like him, when I viewed the bliss of my protectors, the bitter gall of envy rose within me.'** *(Chapter 15)* When he reads Victor's account of his creation **'in language which painted your own horrors, and rendered mine indelible'**, as he tells Victor, he curses the creator who abandoned him *(Chapter 15)*.

The incidents that change him appear to be first his rejection and abandonment by the family he thought of as his 'protectors', which leads him to burn down their cottage, and his wounding by the man whose sweetheart he saves from drowning: **'The feelings of kindness and gentleness, which I had entertained but a few moments before, gave place to hellish rage and gnashing of teeth. Inflamed by pain, I vowed eternal hatred and vengeance to all mankind.'** *(Chapter 16)* When William tells him his father is a Frankenstein, the rage and revenge spill over to encompass not only the child, but also Justine, who reminds him of the loving companion he can never have.

The creature wants Victor to make him such a companion. He promises they will live far away from human society and cause no harm. He describes a life similar to the Garden of Eden: **'My food is not that of man; I do not destroy the lamb and the kid to glut my appetite; acorns and berries afford me sufficient nourishment. My companion will be of the same nature as myself, and will be content with the same fare. We shall make our bed of dried leaves; the sun will shine on us as on man, and ripen our food.'** *(Chapter 17)*

The creature has a dual nature which both mirrors and exaggerates human beings, as his physical stature does. He is physically superior but of a hideous appearance, he is compassionate and vengeful, he is rational and passionate, and he lives alone but is desperate for love and companionship. He is much like other human beings and therefore reflects both Adam and Satan, except for his apparently supernatural powers of climbing and running, and his uncanny ability to track down his victims.

The creature is bound to Victor, as any child to its parent, despite his rejection and cannot harm his creator however much he rages. He takes his revenge for the destruction of his mate by murdering those who Victor loves, starting with Henry Clerval, until Victor is as solitary and alone as the creature himself. The two of them are linked in a final duel for survival. Instead of following Victor, the creature now leads him across the continent into the Arctic.

Although he can be seen as driving Victor to his death, the creature still grieves for him, as Walton observes. He tells Walton that he need not fear any further harm as he is going out into the Arctic wasteland to die. **'I shall ascend my funeral pile triumphantly, and exult in the agony of the torturing flames. The light of that conflagration will fade away; my ashes will be swept into the sea by the winds.'** *(Chapter 24)* With that he springs out of the cabin window and is carried away into the distant darkness. It is an appropriately lonely end for a creature who lived a solitary life.

Key quotations

Once I falsely hoped to meet with beings, who, pardoning my outward form, would love me for the excellent qualities which I was capable of unfolding. I was nourished with high thoughts of honour and devotion. But now crime has degraded me beneath the meanest animal.
(Chapter 24)

Activity 2

Look at the creature's presentation in the novel.

a) Find all the evidence that suggests it was kind and gentle and wanted to do the right thing.

b) Find all the evidence that suggests it was evil, and full of envy and spite, and wanted to destroy things.

c) Compare your findings and put them onto a sheet of paper (you could group them round a picture of the creature if you wish). Give your sheet a suitable title and share it with your classmates.

Robert Walton

He is the first character we meet in the story and his narrative encompasses the others. He is important both as a recorder of everything told to him by Victor and as a witness to Victor's end and the creature's reaction to it. His letters to his sister tell of his voyage to the Arctic Ocean with the intention of finding the North Pole and the Northwest passage, and of his rescue of Victor.

He had a neglected education for which he tries to compensate by extensive reading (much like Mary Shelley and the creature). Like her, he is fascinated by *The Rime of the Ancient Mariner*, which inspired his desire for Arctic exploration. He prepared himself by working as a seaman on Greenland whaling ships where **'my captain offered me the second dignity in the vessel, and entreated me to remain with the greatest earnestness; so valuable did he consider my services'** *(Letter 1)*. This suggests he has sound common sense, in addition to burning ambition, a quality Victor seems to lack.

Walton also has similarities to Victor. He is obsessive in his pursuit of knowledge: **'I shall satiate my ardent curiosity with the sight of a part of the world never before visited, and may tread a land never before imprinted by the foot of man.'** *(Letter 1)* He also wants to penetrate the mysteries of Nature by discovering the secrets of the magnetic pole and he dreams, like Victor, of earning fame and gratitude: **'... you cannot contest the inestimable benefit which I shall confer on all mankind to the last generation, by discovering a passage near the pole to those countries, to reach which at present so many months are requisite; or by ascertaining the secret of the magnet, which, if at all possible, can only be effected by an undertaking such as mine.'** *(Letter 1)* He even asserts that he would sacrifice everything for his enterprise. Recognizing this fatal ambition is what prompts Victor to tell his own story as a warning.

Walton can also be compared to the creature in his feelings of loneliness and desire for a companion. While recognizing the qualities of his lieutenant and the master of his ship, he desires **'the company of a man who could sympathise with me; whose eyes would reply to mine'** *(Letter 2)*. In Victor, he finds such a man although, unlike Victor, who tells no one of his plans to create a human, he wants a friend who thinks as he does **'to approve or amend my plans'** *(Letter 2)*. In fact he doesn't follow Victor's advice to continue his voyage – in the face of the crew's determination to return home, he gives in and agrees to abandon it. He feels ashamed but readers may see it as a victory for common sense. Perhaps his fondness for *The Ancient Mariner* acts as a warning about going against the crew and against Nature. He claims, **'I come back ignorant and disappointed'** *(Chapter 24)*, but he has actually learned more about himself in his weeks embedded in the ice than Victor seems to have learned in a number of years. He takes the feelings and wishes of others into consideration, which Victor seldom does.

Walton seems fond of his sister and anxious to impress her. He confides in her all his feelings, hopes, fears and ambitions, as well as the progress of his voyage and the events that happen to him. It is Walton who finally sees the creature and talks to him, so the reader knows what happens in the end. He is the only person to share the creature's sense of loss at Victor's death. He writes to Margaret, **'what comment can I make on the untimely extinction of this glorious spirit?'** *(Chapter 24)* He hears the creature address Victor's dead body: **'Oh, Frankenstein! generous and self-devoted being!'** *(Chapter 24)*

Mary Shelley's presentation of Walton as a primary narrator who can understand both Victor and his creature gives a sense of reality to an extraordinary tale.

By being more down to earth and mature than either, he survives to journey home and tell the tale and, 'while I am wafted towards England, and towards you, I will not despond' *(Chapter 24)*. He is similar to Victor, but with a sense of responsibility, and is mature enough to know when he has gone too far.

Key quotations

Be assured, that for my own sake, as well as yours, I will not rashly encounter danger. I will be cool, persevering, and prudent. *(Letter 3)*

But success shall crown my endeavours. Wherefore not? Thus far I have gone, tracing a secure way over the pathless seas: the very stars themselves being witnesses and testimonies of my triumph. Why not still proceed over the untamed yet obedient element? What can stop the determined heart and resolved will of man? *(Letter 3)*

Activity 3

Look at the two key quotations above. Think about how they show the two sides of Walton's character – pragmatic and ambitious. What other evidence can you find of these opposing qualities?

- Examine Walton's relationship with his sister, from his letters.

- Look at his relationship with Victor Frankenstein.

Henry Clerval

Victor met Henry, the son of a local merchant, at school and they became close friends: 'He was a boy of singular talent and fancy. He loved enterprise, hardship, and even danger, for its own sake. He was deeply read in books of chivalry and romance. He composed heroic songs, and began to write many a tale of enchantment and knightly adventure.' *(Chapter 2)* He has different interests from Victor and yet both of them were inspired to ambitions that would benefit mankind.

Mary Shelley presents Henry as the person who might have had a restraining influence on Frankenstein's obsession, but then makes it impossible for him to accompany Victor to Ingolstadt. Despite all his pleading, Henry's father refuses to allow him to become a student for he 'was a narrow-minded trader, and saw idleness and ruin in the aspirations and ambition of his son' *(Chapter 3)*. Of course if Henry had gone with Victor there would not have been a story.

Dramatically, Mary Shelley times Henry's arrival in Ingolstadt, having finally persuaded his father to let him go, with Victor's flight from his newly created monster. In one of the novel's many coincidences the coach bringing Henry arrives just where Victor is standing: 'Nothing could equal my delight on seeing Clerval; his presence brought back to my thoughts my father, Elizabeth, and all those scenes of home so dear to my recollection.' *(Chapter 5)* All Victor tells about his shocking work, however, in answer to Henry's concern about his poorly looks is, '**I have lately been so deeply engaged in one occupation, that I have not allowed myself sufficient rest…**' *(Chapter 5)* and he gives his friend no opportunity to question him further before succumbing to a 'nervous fever', which Henry devotedly nurses him through. Henry proves himself a true friend by delaying his own studies to look after Victor and write letters to his family.

Henry is a kind and empathetic man, sensitive to the feelings of others. Victor tells us that his '**eyes and feelings were always quick in discerning the sensations of others**' *(Chapter 6)*. When he sees that Victor is uncomfortable near the room that had been his laboratory, he changes his apartment and he turns the subject away from Natural Philosophy because he observes Frankenstein's agitation. In return he receives no confidence from his friend: '… **although I loved him with mixture of affection and reverence that knew no bounds, yet I could never persuade myself to confide to him that event that was so often present to my recollection, but which I feared the detail to another would only impress more deeply**' *(Chapter 6)*.

Henry begins to study 'Persian, Arabic and Sanscrit' and Victor joins him, finding the studies soothing. Later they go on a walking tour around Ingolstadt and Henry '**again taught me to love the aspect of nature, and the cheerful faces of children**' *(Chapter 6)*. The news of William's murder takes Victor back to Geneva and the reader does not meet Henry again until he and Victor meet up in Germany on their way to England. Henry is full of the joy of life, falling in love with the country along the Rhine, while Victor broods on his promise to the creature. Victor tells us that he has a goal in mind: '**His design was to visit India, in the belief that he had in his knowledge of its various languages, and in the views he had taken of its society, the means of materially assisting the progress of European colonisation and trade.**' *(Chapter 19)*

After visits to towns such as Oxford and Edinburgh, Victor parts from Henry at Perth, wanting to be alone to complete the creature's mate as he promised. The next we hear of Henry is that he has been murdered by the creature after Victor's destruction of the promised partner, and Victor is arrested for the crime. Henry's death is the first in the creature's final revenge.

Mary Shelley makes Henry a **foil** to Frankenstein. He is frank and honest, where Victor is secretive and deceptive; he is open and generous, while Victor is selfish and thoughtless; and Henry is modest and eager to learn from others, whereas Victor is arrogant and obsessively exclusive in his research. Although both men die before their time, Henry's death inspires sympathy in the reader, while Victor's seems both inevitable and self-induced.

> **foil** a character that contrasts with another in order to show up certain qualities or failings

> **Key quotations**
>
> He was a being formed in the 'very poetry of nature'. His wild and
> enthusiastic imagination was chastened by the sensibility of his heart.
> His soul overflowed with ardent affections, and his friendship was of
> that devoted and wondrous nature that the worldly-minded teach us to
> look for only in the imagination. *(Chapter 18)*

Activity 4

a) Discuss or consider what the novel would lose if the character of Henry Clerval
was omitted. You should consider the following episodes in particular:

- the childhood friendship between Henry and Victor
- Henry's arrival in Ingolstadt just after the creature's creation
- the walking tour of the Ingolstadt area shortly before William's murder
- the tour of the Rhine en route for England
- the two friends' tour of England and Scotland
- Henry's murder.

b) Create a presentation to show your findings. You should include your own
thoughts and ideas, supported by quotations. You could add pictures and
captions to make your presentation more attractive. Show it to your classmates
and invite feedback.

Elizabeth Lavenza

'When my father returned from Milan, he found playing with me in the hall of
our villa, a child fairer than pictured cherub – a creature who seemed to shed
radiance from her looks, and whose form and motions were lighter than the
chamois of the hills.' *(Chapter 2)* This description of Elizabeth introduces a being
who seems impossibly perfect. She is presented to Victor by his mother as a **'pretty
present'** and that is how she seems to be treated. She possesses all the virtues
seen as 'womanly' in Mary Shelley's time and by making her such an angelic and
compliant figure the author invites us to consider how women were regarded.

Elizabeth is saved from dying by the sacrifice of Victor's mother Caroline, whose
deathbed wish is for her to marry Victor. She takes over Caroline's duties as a
mother to the younger boys without complaint. 'She looked steadily on life, and
assumed its duties with courage and zeal. She devoted herself to those
whom she had been taught to call her uncle and cousins.' *(Chapter 3)*

She writes letters to Frankenstein and it is this correspondence that reveals the story of Justine Moritz, which prepares the reader for her later role in William's death.

Elizabeth is the most patient and faithful of women, writing constantly to Victor and never reproaching him despite his neglect of her. She shows courage and loyalty in her defence of Justine, when everyone believes her guilty of William's murder. Unlike Victor, and without his evidence, she speaks up for Justine in court, although her words merely make things worse. Justine's death, even more than William's, destroys Elizabeth's happiness and belief in justice. Elizabeth puts everyone else before herself, trying to console Victor, although ignorant of what is causing his despair.

Victor treats Elizabeth almost as his property, telling his father she has **'my warmest admiration and affection'** *(Chapter 18)*, which hardly sounds as if he is overcome with passion. She is spoken of in the language of ownership. He promises her to himself as a 'reward' and 'consolation', which follows from the 'pretty present' he received as a child. When he has made the creature's mate and got rid of the creature, he will 'claim' her, like a lottery prize. If he manages to destroy the

creature '... **in my Elizabeth I possessed a treasure'** *(Chapter 22)*. For her part, Elizabeth is so selfless that she even writes to him as he returns from Scotland, offering to break their engagement if he has any doubts because she loves him in a way he can never love her.

Her reward for all this is that he will, after they are married, tell her the dreadful secret he has been keeping. By then, of course, it will be too late for her to break the engagement and she will have no warning of the creature's promise to be with Victor on his wedding night. Sadly, Elizabeth is so lacking in a real personality that the reader can feel little sorrow at her death.

Victor finally claims Elizabeth, the 'ideal woman', as his reward, with little thought for her safety

Key quotations

The saintly soul of Elizabeth shone like a shrine-dedicated lamp in our peaceful home. Her sympathy was ours; her smile, her soft voice, the sweet glance of her celestial eyes, were ever there to bless and animate us. She was the living spirit of love to soften and attract... *(Chapter 2)*

Activity 5

We only see Elizabeth through Victor's narration and her occasional letters. Consider the following phrases from the key quotation above and what they suggest about Victor's view of Elizabeth:

- saintly soul

- shrine-dedicated lamp

- celestial eyes

- living spirit of love.

Write two or three paragraphs describing how Mary Shelley presents Elizabeth and what you consider to be her role in the novel.

Justine Moritz

Although a servant, Justine is like one of the family and devoted to Caroline Frankenstein, who saved her from a tyrannical mother. Elizabeth describes her in a letter: 'Justine was the most grateful little creature in the world... you could see by her eyes that she almost adored her protectress.' *(Chapter 6)* In addition to being grateful, Justine is shown to be patient and long suffering in her attention to her own mother after the rest of her family died. She wins Elizabeth's love because she reminds her of Caroline in her speech and manners.

This description prepares the reader for the Frankenstein family's inability to believe that Justine murdered William, a belief confirmed by Victor, although he still doesn't tell the truth that might have saved her from the hangman. It seems odd that when he tells his brother Ernest, "You are all mistaken; I know the murderer" *(Chapter 7)*, Ernest doesn't question him further and Victor then thinks better of his impulse to confess.

Justine is a victim who does not help her own cause. When she gives her explanation in court about what happened, she says she spent the night in a barn rather than call on the house where she was known (and would have been provided with an alibi). She further says that, although she has no idea how the miniature came into her pocket, "I believe that I have no enemy on earth, and none surely would have been so wicked as to destroy me wantonly. Did the murderer place it there? I know of no opportunity afforded him for so doing; or, if I had, why should he have stolen the jewel, to part with it again so soon?" *(Chapter 8)* It seems almost as though she wishes to be convicted. When she then allows herself to be bullied into confessing, the outcome is certain, unless Victor tells the truth.

Mary Shelley presents Justine as a martyr to Victor's cowardice and egotism, as well as a victim of the monster he created. She is a **symbol** of innocence, suffering because of others' evil actions. She is also presented as the victim of the Catholic Church, since it is her priest who threatens her with hell to make her confess. She does not have great depth as a character, but represents patient resignation in the face of death: **"In these last moments I feel the sincerest gratitude towards those who think of me with kindness. How sweet is the affection of others to such a wretch as I am!"** *(Chapter 8)* Her function in the novel is to add to the moral debate about responsibility and blame.

Key quotations

"I do not fear to die... God raises my weakness, and gives me courage to endure the worst. I leave a sad and bitter world; and if you remember me, and think of me as one unjustly condemned, I am resigned to the fate awaiting me. Learn from me, dear lady, to submit in patience to the will of Heaven!" *(Chapter 8)*

Activity 6

In a small group, discuss who has the final responsibility for Justine's death. Each person could take one of the following views:

- It is the fault of the priest who forced her to confess.
- It is the fault of the court for not investigating properly.
- It is Justine's own fault for making a poor case for herself and then confessing.
- It is the fault of the creature, who murdered William and planted the evidence on Justine.
- It is the fault of Victor for creating the creature and then not telling anyone who was the real murderer.

You should organize this like a debate and make sure you support your viewpoint with relevant references and quotations.

---

symbol something that represents ideas beyond itself, as a flag is a symbol of a country or the colour white stands for purity

Alphonse Frankenstein

Victor tells us, '… **my father had filled several public situations with honour and reputation. He was respected by all who knew him, for his integrity and indefatigable attention to public business. He passed his younger days perpetually occupied by the affairs of his country**' *(Chapter 1)*. The result of this dedication is that Alphonse married late in life. He seems to be a caring and loving parent whose '**smile of benevolent pleasure while regarding me**' is one of Victor's earliest memories *(Chapter 1)*. He sees his parents as '**the agents and creators of all the many delights which we enjoyed**' *(Chapter 2)*. This does not stop Victor blaming his father for not explaining '**that the principles of Agrippa had been entirely exploded**', which he would then have instantly discarded: '**It is even possible, that the train of my ideas would never have received the fatal impulse that led to my ruin.**' *(Chapter 2)* Blaming his father for his later creation of the creature is typical of Victor's desire to evade responsibility, even though his father might have helped by explaining a little more.

Alphonse is patient and continues to write when Victor neglects to write letters to him. Victor only takes notice of the letter telling him of William's death, which finally takes him home to Geneva to hear of Justine's arrest. Unfortunately, Alphonse has a misplaced faith in the judicial system which makes Victor decide he doesn't need to confess: '**If she is, as you believe, innocent, rely on the justice of our laws, and the activity with which I shall prevent the slightest shadow of partiality.**' *(Chapter 7)*

Despite his advancing years, Alphonse travels to Scotland to nurse Victor through his illness in prison, following Henry's murder. After Victor's acquittal, his father tries to cheer him up by referring to home and Elizabeth. However, Victor wants to return to Geneva merely to try and protect his family from the creature – but without telling them of the danger they are in. Alphonse worries about his son and urges him towards marriage with Elizabeth, unaware how fatal it will be. He tells Victor, '**Heavy misfortunes have befallen us; but let us only cling closer to what remains, and transfer our love for those whom we have lost, to those who yet live.**' *(Chapter 22)* Elizabeth's death proves too much for him and he dies in Victor's arms.

Mary Shelley presents Alphonse as a good father for his time, kind and loving, and, by implication, worthy of a better life than Victor has allowed him through his arrogant folly and continued deceit. Like Justine, Alphonse is indirectly killed by the creature Victor creates and this contributes to the moral tale of responsibility.

Key quotations

Come, Victor; not brooding thoughts of vengeance against the assassin, but with feelings of peace and gentleness, that will heal, instead of festering, the wounds of our minds. Enter the house of mourning, my friend, but with kindness and affection for those who love you, and not with hatred for your enemies. *(Chapter 7)*

Caroline Frankenstein

'... Caroline Beaufort possessed a mind of an uncommon mould; and her courage rose to support her in her adversity. She procured plain work; she plaited straw; and by various means contrived to earn a pittance scarcely sufficient to support life' *(Chapter 1)*. Like Elizabeth and Justine, Caroline is both a victim and an angel – beautiful, loving, hard-working and generous. Like them, she also needs a man to rescue her, in this case, Alphonse, who 'came like a protecting spirit to the poor girl, who committed herself to his care' *(Chapter 1)*.

We learn little about Caroline except that she was devoted to her husband and children, including Elizabeth whose life she saved at the expense of her own. She is thus presented by Mary Shelley as a true martyr. Knowing her death is near, she begs Elizabeth to take her place as mother to the younger boys. Her final action is to ensure that Victor and Elizabeth will be married, so keeping things in the family. This is confirmed by Victor's later dream, in which Elizabeth turns into his dead mother.

Key quotations

It was an historical subject, painted at my father's desire, and represented Caroline Beaufort in an agony of despair, kneeling by the coffin of her dead father. Her garb was rustic, and her cheek pale; but there was an air of dignity and beauty, that hardly permitted the sentiment of pity. *(Chapter 7)*

Activity 7

Imagine that you have been asked to write an obituary for Victor's parents for a national newspaper. Find examples of newspaper obituary pages to give you the correct format. You should include the following:

- names, ages (make them up) and where they lived

- the surviving family members and their relationships to the deceased

- any positions that were held and particular interests

- something about their personalities, along with any anecdotes that give an idea of their characters

- cause of death

- short quotations from the novel where appropriate.

The De Lacey family

Their story is at the heart of the novel and they represent the best aspects of humanity. The old man is gentle, uncomplaining and the only person to react kindly to the creature, since he is blind and unprejudiced by appearance. The son and daughter look after their father lovingly, and are hard-working and kind to each other. Despite their poverty – caused by their support of Safie's father, who betrayed them – they are generous: **'The poor that stopped at their door were never driven away.'** *(Chapter 15)*

Through them the creature learns the values of family life: **'The gentle manners and beauty of the cottagers greatly endeared them to me: when they were unhappy, I felt depressed; when they rejoiced, I sympathised in their joys.'** *(Chapter 12)* From them he learns how to be caring. When he discovers they are unhappy through poverty, he stops stealing food from them and helps them by collecting wood and clearing snow. He is also impressed by their good looks, which are such a contrast with his own reflection.

Mary Shelley presents this family as ideal – they are well born, handsome, caring and affectionate as well as being educated and thoughtful. They are given names that mean 'happiness' (Felix) and 'good' (Agatha). Nevertheless they show prejudice and harshness towards the creature, simply because of his appearance. In this respect they are no different to the other humans he encounters. If even people like them cannot give the creature sympathy, it is not surprising that he wants a mate with whom he can turn his back on humans and live in exile.

Although Agatha is very similar to Mary Shelley's other female characters, Safie is different. She is strong-willed enough to disobey her father and ignore his instructions to follow him home. Instead she has the courage to choose freedom in a foreign land where she doesn't speak the language and she sets out to find Felix. Her arrival is the cause of rejoicing in the De Lacey family and the language lessons she receives from Felix benefit the creature as well. Safie brings money with her so that **'Felix and Agatha spent more time in amusement and conversation, and were assisted in their labours by servants.'** *(Chapter 15)* Mary Shelley has chosen to put Safie's story at the very centre of the novel, which suggests that her creation of this strong independent-minded woman has some importance.

> **Key quotations**
>
> The more I saw of them, the greater became my desire to claim their protection and kindness; my heart yearned to be known and loved by these amiable creatures: to see their sweet looks directed towards me with affection, was the utmost limit of my ambition. *(Chapter 15)*

Activity 8

a) Make a list of the ways in which Safie is different from Caroline Frankenstein, Elizabeth Lavenza, Justine Moritz and Agatha De Lacey. You should consider:

- their relationships with men
- the way they spend their days
- their place in domestic life
- their upbringing and education.

b) Why do you think Mary Shelley has included Safie in the novel? What would the narrative of the De Lacey family lose without it? What would the novel's general view of women be without her? Write a paragraph on your view of Safie's role in the novel.

Margaret Saville

Although we never see her, Margaret is a presence in the novel as Robert Walton's sister and correspondent. We are made aware that she does not approve of Walton's expedition, for almost the first thing he does is reassure her that **'no disaster has accompanied the commencement of an enterprise which you have regarded with such evil forebodings'** *(Letter 1)*. He also seeks her good opinion, for he asks, **'do I not deserve to accomplish some great purpose?'** *(Letter 1)* He expresses love and gratitude towards her but, rather like an immature youth, wants her to worry about him as well: **'If I succeed, many, many months, perhaps years, will pass before you and I may meet…'** *(Letter 1)*.

He also enjoys the thought of her reactions to Frankenstein's story, which will make **'your blood congeal with horror'** *(Chapter 24)*. Nevertheless by the end of his account he is looking forward to receiving her consolation when he reaches England. She is important because she occupies the same position as the novel's readers, as Walton's letters unfold the story and Walton says that he **'may receive your letters on some occasions when I need them most to support my spirits'** *(Letter 2)*.

Walton's care for Margaret and his anxiety for her good opinion is in contrast to Victor's disregard for his family when he becomes obsessed with his research. It may be this bond that prevents Walton making the same errors as Victor.

Minor characters

M. Krempe is Professor of Natural Philosophy at Ingolstadt University: **'a little squat man, with a gruff voice and a repulsive countenance'.** *(Chapter 3)* Victor, who judges so much by appearances, is naturally repelled from his subject.

M. Waldman, on the other hand, who is the Chemistry Professor, **'appeared about fifty years of age, but with an aspect expressive of the greatest benevolence; a few grey hairs covered his temples, but those at the back of his head were nearly black. His person was short, but remarkably erect; and his voice the sweetest I had ever heard.'** *(Chapter 3)* It is his words and behaviour that set Victor on the path to discovering the principle of life, with such dire results.

Mr Kirwin is the Scottish magistrate, 'an old benevolent man, with calm and mild manners' *(Chapter 21)*. He arranges for Victor to see the body of Henry Clerval and arranges nursing care for him when he becomes ill. He is kind enough to write to Victor's father in Geneva, telling him of his son's condition and arranging for him to see Victor.

Mary Shelley includes each of these characters to advance the plot. They act as agents by which Victor arrives at the knowledge that enables him to create the creature and, later, to recover after his broken promise results in Henry's murder.

Writing about characters

Upgrade

You may be asked to answer a question about a character or a group of characters from the novel. You will need to show your knowledge of each one not just as a person, but as a created character with a specific role or function in the story. You will need to cover the following in your answer:

- the kinds of things the author gives the character to say and how they say them
- the kinds of things the author gives the character to do and how they do them
- what the author makes the narrator tell us about the character
- how the author makes other characters react to them
- why the author has included the character in the novel (their role or function).

You will need to give detailed evidence from the novel to support all the points you make, including quotations where appropriate.

Character map

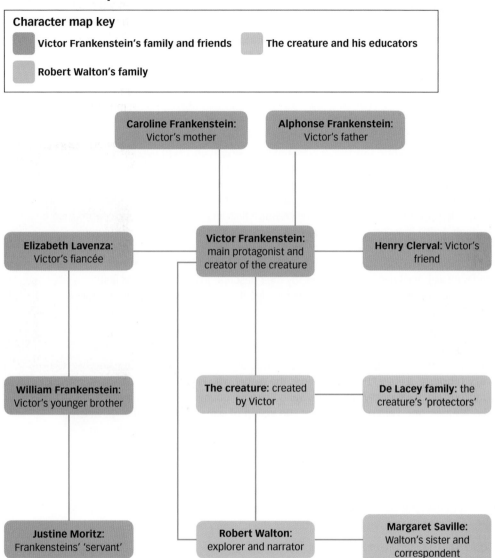

Character map key

Victor Frankenstein's family and friends

The creature and his educators

Robert Walton's family

Caroline Frankenstein: Victor's mother

Alphonse Frankenstein: Victor's father

Elizabeth Lavenza: Victor's fiancée

Victor Frankenstein: main protagonist and creator of the creature

Henry Clerval: Victor's friend

William Frankenstein: Victor's younger brother

The creature: created by Victor

De Lacey family: the creature's 'protectors'

Justine Moritz: Frankensteins' 'servant'

Robert Walton: explorer and narrator

Margaret Saville: Walton's sister and correspondent

Narration

Although Mary Shelley uses three different narrators to tell her story, their language has similarities, especially in the use of **elevated diction** and **rhetoric**. For example, Robert Walton describes his exploration of the Arctic wastes as: **'There is something at work in my soul... there is a love for the marvellous, a belief in the marvellous, intertwined in all my projects, which hurries me out of the common pathways of men, even to the wild sea and unvisited regions I am about to explore.'** *(Letter 2)* Victor Frankenstein refers to his studies at Ingolstadt in similar terms: **'None but those who have experienced them can conceive of the enticements of science. In other studies you go as far as others have gone before you, and there is no more to know; but in a scientific pursuit there is continual food for discovery and wonder.'** *(Chapter 4)* As if to underline his similarity to the other narrators, the creature tells Victor: **'While I improved in speech, I also learned the science of letters, as it was taught to the stranger; and this opened before me a wide field for wonder and delight.'** *(Chapter 13)* Mary Shelley links the narrators' shared enthusiasm for exploration, whether geographical, scientific or educational, by their description of it. The use of first-person narratives means the reader has to judge the reliability of each narrator for themselves, especially of Walton, who has overall control of the story.

Another feature of the narratives is the way they refer back to the narrator at intervals, as if to ensure there is no confusion about who is the storyteller at this point. Robert Walton's letters refer to his sister, with phrases such as **'I love you very tenderly'** *(Letter 2)*, which reminds the reader who is writing them. Victor Frankenstein occasionally addresses Walton directly during his story, with comments like, **'Remember, I am not recording the vision of a madman'** *(Chapter 4)*, which reminds us that this tale is being recounted face to face. The creature, in his own narrative, reminds Victor of the papers that recorded his creation, saying, **"You, doubtless, recollect these papers."** *(Chapter 15)* This kind of intervention reminds the reader of the circumstances in which the story is being related. It is also a way of giving credibility to a fantastic tale, in the same way as the creature gives Victor copies of the letters written to Felix by Safie, saying **'... they will prove the truth of my tale'** *(Chapter 14)*. Victor, in turn, passes them to Walton for the same purpose.

Letters also occur within Frankenstein's narrative, giving a voice to other characters, such as his father and Elizabeth. These letters are mainly used to further the plot, like Victor's father writing of William's death, or to give background information, such as Elizabeth's account of the story of Justine Moritz.

Mary Shelley's narrative style also uses **apostrophe**. In his recorded narrative, Victor has a habit of addressing Nature as well as people: **"Dear Mountains! my own beautiful lake! how do you welcome your wanderer?"** *(Chapter 7)* Later, after hearing the creature's tale, he cries out, **"Oh! stars and clouds, and winds, ye are all about to mock me..."** *(Chapter 17)*. The creature cries out, **"Oh, Frankenstein!**

generous and self-devoted being!" to the corpse of his creator *(Chapter 24)*. This act of addressing something inanimate gives it a powerful human quality that suggests understanding in things that cannot possess it – a form of **personification**. Here it implies that these natural phenomena are like friends or enemies.

The creature laments the death of Victor Frankenstein in the 1994 film *Mary Shelley's Frankenstein*

The text is also full of exclamations, intended to provide emphasis, as when Ernest tells Victor that the murderer of William has been found: '**The murderer discovered! Good God! how can that be?**' *(Chapter 7)* The creature's horror after reading Victor's notes on his making is expressed as, "**Hateful day when I received life! ... Accursed creator!**" *(Chapter 15)* These exclamations are generally used in moments of extreme emotion. Sometimes they stress warmer feelings, such as Victor's '**Sweet and beloved Elizabeth!**' *(Chapter 22)*, although this is uttered under the threat of the creature's appearance on their wedding night. Modern writers use few or no exclamation marks, but Mary Shelley and her contemporaries used them for added drama.

The author also uses rhetorical questions as a technique whereby characters explain their motives, e.g. when Walton writes to his sister, '**Why not still proceed over the untamed yet obedient element? What can stop the determined heart and resolved will of man?**' *(Letter 3)* When Victor evades his responsibility for Justine, he asks himself, '**Did anyone indeed exist, except I, the creator, who would believe, unless his senses convinced him, in the existence of the living**

apostrophe a rhetorical device whereby an abstract thing or a dead person is addressed in order to give emotional emphasis

elevated diction formal, high level vocabulary

personification giving human attributes or characteristics to inanimate or abstract things

rhetoric the conscious use of eloquence (fluent or persuasive language) to influence an audience

monument of presumption and rash ignorance which I had let loose upon the world?' *(Chapter 7)* The creature, when he is telling Victor how he was driven from the De Lacey's cottage, also says, 'Why, in that instant, did I not extinguish the spark of existence which you had so wantonly bestowed?' *(Chapter 16)*

How far each of these narrators is reliable is left to the reader to decide. Robert Walton makes no secret of his admiration and even affection for Victor Frankenstein, yet still says that the letters he was shown and his sighting of the creature were greater proof that the story was true. Frankenstein himself tells his story seemingly both to warn Walton and to excuse his actions. Mary Shelley provides ample evidence of his character and unreliability in the tone he adopts and the light in which he regards his actions. It is he who reports the creature's tale and that he does so faithfully we can judge by the sympathy we feel for him and by his own words to Walton at the end of the novel.

Activity 1

a) Discuss and make notes on the following, finding one or two quotations to support your ideas:

- What does the reader learn of Walton's purpose for his journey?
- What do you learn about the crew that Walton hires in Archangel?
- What is Walton's impression of the man he rescues from the ice?

b) Write a paragraph giving your views of Robert Walton as a narrator of the main story.

Activity 2

a) Find quotations that are typical of the way in which the following characters address each other:

- Victor Frankenstein and the creature
- Robert Walton and Victor Frankenstein
- Victor Frankenstein and Henry Clerval.

What do you notice about the words used in each case?

b) What is Mary Shelley trying to tell the reader about each of these relationships through her choice of language and form of address?

Foreshadowing

Mary Shelley uses foreshadowing throughout the novel as a technique for introducing suspense. Soon after Victor has been rescued by Walton, he reacts to the Captain's recital of his ambitions by groaning, "Unhappy man! Do you share my madness? Have you drank also of the intoxicating draught? Hear me, –

let me reveal my tale, and you will dash the cup from your lips!" *(Letter 4)* Not surprisingly this makes both Walton and the reader very anxious to find out the cause of this outburst. Again, at the end of Chapter 2, Victor tells us, '**It was a strong effort of the spirit of good; but it was ineffectual. Destiny was too potent, and her immutable laws had decreed my utter and terrible destruction.**' This tells the reader that something very bad is going to happen later on, although without giving much idea what it will be. The idea of 'destiny' or fate being in control implies that Victor will be powerless to alter it, although this is a false trail, as we later learn.

Meanwhile it encourages the reader to continue in order to find out what happens. This is reinforced again when Victor is wandering around the scene of William's death and reflects, '**The picture appeared a vast and dim scene of evil, and I foresaw obscurely that I was destined to become the most wretched of human beings.**' *(Chapter 7)* Later, after the disastrous creation of the creature, Victor has a prophetic dream in which Elizabeth turns into his mother's corpse as he embraces her, thus ironically foretelling the death and decay that Victor's pursuit of the principles of life will cause. The reader now has some inkling that Elizabeth may be in future danger, which they may remember later when the creature promises to be with Victor on his wedding night.

Victor occasionally breaks off from his narration to make a comment that tells the reader what happens further on in his story. When describing his travels down the Rhine with Henry Clerval, for example, he digresses into a reflection on his friend: '**And where does he now exist? Is this gentle and lovely being lost for ever? … Does it now only exist in my memory?**' *(Chapter 18)* This arouses the reader's interest in Clerval's fate and makes them keen to learn how he meets his end.

Mary Shelley uses foreshadowing with great effect in the repetition of the creature's threat, "**I shall be with you on your wedding night**" *(Chapter 20)*. Victor tells us, '**Great God! if for one instant I had thought what might be the hellish intention of my fiendish adversary, I would rather have banished myself for ever from my native country**' *(Chapter 22)*. The reader, however, is likely to be ahead of him.

Activity 3

The use of tension and suspense is a device to keep people reading the story, just as the back cover text and advertisements are designed to make people want to read the novel in the first place.

a) Write new text for the back cover of *Frankenstein* that you think will persuade your age group to read the novel.

b) Design a magazine advertisement for *Frankenstein* that you think will sell the novel to teenagers. Try to include at least one or two quotations that will act as selling points.

Allusion

One of the ways Mary Shelley uses her story is as a creation myth, which is articulated by the creature himself when he discovers *Paradise Lost*. When he meets with Victor on the mountain, he tells him, **"Remember, that I am thy creature; I ought to be thy Adam; but I am rather the fallen angel, whom thou drivest from joy for no misdeed."** *(Chapter 10)* He refers constantly to Victor as his 'creator', often qualified by 'cursed', and the suggestion is that, in contrast to Adam, he was made to be cursed rather than blessed. This idea is supported by the creature's identification with Satan (the fallen angel) in *Paradise Lost*, which the reader notes when he compares the shepherd's hut with the capital of hell in *Paradise Lost*: '**... it presented to me then as exquisite and divine a retreat as Pandaemonium appeared to the demons of hell after their sufferings in the lake of fire**' *(Chapter 11)*. Later the creature comments that even Satan was better off, having company in his hell.

Victor also compares himself with Adam in the loss of Paradise through forbidden knowledge. On his way home to Elizabeth he reflects, '**the apple was already eaten, and the angel's arm bared to drive me from all hope**' *(Chapter 22)*. The reader might also be tempted to compare him with Satan as his arrogance drives him to challenge God as the creator.

The subtitle to the novel is 'The modern Prometheus'. This also refers to a creation myth, although classical rather than biblical. Prometheus was said to have created the human race and later stolen fire from the gods to benefit humans, as referred to in the creature's account of his discovery of fire in Chapter 11. Victor says he intends to benefit mankind by creating a new race of beings and then working to abolish death. Prometheus was punished by Zeus for stealing fire with the eternal torment of having an eagle tear at his liver, as he lay chained to a rock (the liver renewed each night, since he was immortal). Victor is punished by the loss of all those he loves as well as any possible peace of mind. He even exclaims, when he is ill, after Clerval's murder, '**Of what materials was I made, that I could thus resist so many shocks, which, like the turning of the wheel, continually renewed the torture?**' *(Chapter 21)*

The other main **allusion** Mary Shelley uses is *The Rime of the Ancient Mariner*, the poem responsible for Walton's interest in the Arctic. In the poem, the Mariner is compelled to wander and to tell his story to someone who has no choice but to listen, just as Frankenstein tells his story to Walton. The Mariner's tale concerns an albatross, used as a symbol of love and hope, which he shot down, bringing a

In Coleridge's poem *The Rime of The Ancient Mariner*, the Mariner commits the crime of shooting the albatross with an arrow

curse on himself and the crew. The Mariner survived but all the crew died, in much the same way that Victor lives while all his loved ones are murdered as a result of his arrogance and folly. The Mariner was forced to wear the dead albatross round his neck as a punishment and a symbol of his guilt, just as Victor has to carry the burden of knowledge of what he has done. Victor describes himself in similar terms: **'I wandered like an evil spirit, for I had committed deeds of mischief beyond description horrible'** *(Chapter 9)*. He is also the one who must listen to a tale – in his case the creature's story. The creature is also cursed like the Mariner, but his curse is to have been created as he is: **'the demoniacal corpse to which I had so miserably given life'** *(Chapter 5)*.

Mary Shelley's original readers would have been familiar with these allusions and thus aware of the extra layers of meaning within her story.

> **allusion** reference to another source that may be historical, literary or classical

Activity 4

a) Research these three background tales in the novel, reading a summary and finding out more about each one:

- *Paradise Lost*
- the story of Prometheus
- *The Rime of the Ancient Mariner.*

b) Discuss how Mary Shelley uses these three tales. How do the three main narrators resemble characters in these stories? How and why do they identify with them? What does this use of allusion bring to the novel and what effect does it have on readers?

c) How does allusion fit in with the other language techniques used by Shelley, in your opinion?

Tips for assessment

You do not need to know the texts Mary Shelley uses for allusion in great detail. But you do need to know enough to show that you understand their importance to the text and the extra layers of meaning they bring in terms of:

- universal themes such as good and evil, the loss of innocence, suffering as punishment
- the archetypal characters they refer to, such as the first humans, the idea of a creator god, the devil as tempter, the wanderer/explorer and the storyteller.

Allegory, parable, fairy tale and symbolism

An **allegory** is a story in which characters are used to represent abstract ideas. In *Frankenstein*, while Victor is a real character with thoughts and emotions, he also represents the idea of the 'overreacher' – the one that goes too far and brings disaster to himself and others. His fascination with electrochemistry and his determination to create life lead to his usurping the functions of natural procreation and going against God and Nature. His comparison with Prometheus shows Mary Shelley's intention.

The creature, despite his feelings and intelligence, also represents disorder and chaos, as he is the product of an unnatural process. Despite his comparison with Adam, he is unnaturally large, agile and able to scale mountains at a rapid speed, as well as being impervious to weather. As he comments, having seen his reflection, **'Alas! I did not yet entirely know the fatal effects of this miserable deformity.'** *(Chapter 12)*

Elizabeth stands for the perfect woman of Mary Shelley's society, although she has little individuality. She is beautiful, angelic, endlessly patient and an inevitable victim, as is Justine. Victor's parents are representative of the ideal parents, while Henry Clerval is the perfect friend, although he is also given attributes that make him Victor's opposite: **'Excellent friend! how sincerely you did love me, and endeavour to elevate my mind until it was on a level with your own!'** *(Chapter 6)*

A **parable** is a story with a moral and Frankenstein's reckless flying in the face of Nature brings a terrible revenge. The fairy tale element may be less obvious, until we realize that such tales were often fairly grim in their original versions. They do tell of the fight between good and evil, which is the subject of *Frankenstein*, although it is not always obvious who is good and who is evil. They also contain monsters and elements of the supernatural, which the creature represents. Very often the evil figure in a fairy tale sets the hero or heroine a difficult or impossible task, just as the creature demands that Frankenstein make him a mate. The figures in Mary Shelley's novel are less clear cut. Victor can be seen as evil, since his arrogance and selfishness drive him to create the creature, while the creature can be seen as the victim, wanting to be loved and do good until rejection and hatred turn him towards revenge.

> **allegory** a story with a second meaning, using abstract ideas as personified characters, behind the obvious meaning
>
> **parable** a story related to people's own experiences that illustrates a moral lesson often through personification and/or metaphor

Mary Shelley uses several important symbols in *Frankenstein*. Robert Walton's goal when he sets off on his voyage of exploration is to find the ice and snow of the Arctic. The wasteland there represents death and sterility – a place without warmth, which Walton believes houses **'a land surpassing in wonders and in beauty every region hitherto discovered on the habitable globe'** *(Letter 1)*. It is the final resting place of Victor and of his creature, for whom the ice and snow are of no consequence, except that they create empty spaces. The meeting between Victor and the creature takes place on an empty ice plain, so it seems they can only be together in a place where no life can exist – a pure wasteland that contrasts with the 'workshop of filthy creation' *(Chapter 4)* where the creature was generated.

Another symbol Shelley uses is light, which includes fire. This can be seen as the opposite of ice, since it represents passion and life. It can also, paradoxically, symbolize destruction. This contradiction is expressed by the creature when he first discovers fire: 'I found a fire which had been left by some wandering beggars, and was overcome with delight at the warmth I experienced from it. In my joy I thrust my hand into the live embers, but quickly drew it out again with a cry of pain. How strange, I thought, that the same cause should produce such opposite effects.' *(Chapter 11)* His intention of killing himself on a pyre on the ice brings the creature and Victor together in a final image of destruction.

Light is similarly used both literally and figuratively to express hope and inspiration, or torment and negation. When Victor discovers the elusive principle of life he tells us, 'from the midst of this darkness a sudden light broke in upon me – a light so brilliant and wondrous, yet so simple' *(Chapter 4)*. The absence of light signifies ignorance or depression, as when Victor says, after the death of his father, 'I lost sensation, and chains and darkness were the only objects that pressed upon me.' *(Chapter 23)*

The weather is also used symbolically within the novel, whether it is the lightning strike that begins Victor's interest in science or the thunderstorm that he experiences in the place where William was murdered and makes him exclaim, "William, dear angel! this is thy funeral, this thy dirge!" *(Chapter 7)*, only to see the creature in a flash of lightning.

Activity 5

a) Choose four or five chapters of the novel to focus on. Find examples of Mary Shelley's use of symbolism in your chosen chapters. Make a list under the following categories:

- Light/fire used to show good – warmth, goodness or inspiration
- Light/fire used to show destruction or something bad (e.g. hell)
- Snow/ice used to show barrenness or lack of life
- Snow/ice used to symbolize purity and lack of passion
- The weather used to reflect human moods (pathetic fallacy)
- The weather used as irony – to emphasize the opposite feelings of the person or people involved.

b) Put together a presentation to show Mary Shelley's use of symbolism in *Frankenstein*. You could add pictures, quotations and narrative.

Language and emotions

Romantic writers were drawn to the idea of horror and the gothic, partly because they asserted the primacy of feelings and the subconscious over rationalism and repression.

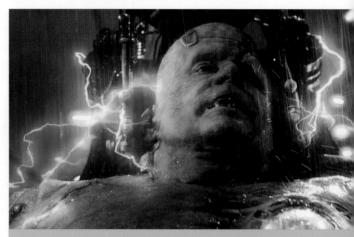

The creature engenders 'breathless horror and disgust' in Victor Frankenstein

In *Frankenstein*, there is some irony in this as Victor the scientist is driven by his emotions, which he often seems unable to express. 'How can I describe my emotions at this catastrophe', he says as the creature is given life, only to tell us in the next paragraph that 'breathless horror and disgust filled my heart' *(Chapter 5)*. Victor's melodramatic utterances continue with phrases such as 'No one can conceive the anguish I suffered' *(Chapter 7)* and 'I cannot pretend to describe what I then felt.' *(Chapter 8)*

This emotive language is used by most of the characters and is intended to draw the reader into the story by sharing, or imagining, their feelings in the situations described. It is not only Victor who says he finds it difficult to express feelings. When he shows Clerval the letter from his father telling of William's death, Henry says, "I can offer you no consolation" *(Chapter 7)*, before expressing his sympathy with some eloquence a paragraph later. Even the creature, who is described by Victor as eloquent, exclaims 'I cannot describe to you the agony that these reflections inflicted upon me' *(Chapter 13)*.

Sometimes emotions are too strong for mere words, as Victor knows after he allows Justine to be hanged: 'I was seized by remorse and the sense of guilt, which hurried me away to a hell of intense tortures, such as no language can describe' *(Chapter 9)*. When Victor leaves for England and Elizabeth says goodbye '– a thousand conflicting emotions rendered her mute, as she bade me a tearful, silent farewell' *(Chapter 18)*.

Most of the characters are also able to describe their emotions with some fluency. Robert Walton writes to his sister about his lack of a friend, 'when I am glowing with the enthusiasm of success, there will be none to participate my joy; if I am assailed by disappointment, no one will endeavour to sustain me in dejection' *(Letter 2)*. This is credible in a letter, where the writer has time to formulate their emotions, but after she is condemned, Justine Moritz tells Elizabeth, "I thought with horror, my sweet lady, that you should believe your Justine, whom your blessed aunt had so highly honoured, and whom you loved, was a creature capable of a crime which none but the devil himself could have perpetrated" *(Chapter 8)*. This language is both emotive and formal, so readers can understand the character's feelings, although it may be surprising that such fluency could be used by someone in such a situation.

Mary Shelley uses highly emotional language to heighten the horror by causing the reader to experience what the characters experience, as far as possible. This language expressing extreme feeling and the use of dreams and the subconscious are factors that place *Frankenstein* in the Romantic and gothic tradition.

Activity 6

a) With a partner, adapt one of the following scenes from the novel for a stage production:

- Chapter 10 where Victor encounters the creature on Montanvert

- Chapter 17 where Victor talks to the creature after hearing his tale

- Chapter 20 where Victor and the creature talk after Victor has destroyed the creature's mate.

Consider where the dialogue refers to emotions and how you could either replace some words with movements and gestures or add to their impact with visual effects.

b) Write two paragraphs about the differences between the way emotions are shown through words alone or in drama.

Figurative language

Mary Shelley makes use of **figurative language** in her novel. She uses personification occasionally, as when Walton writes, **'the very stars themselves being witnesses and testimonies of my triumph'** *(Letter 3)*. Since stars are used as navigation aids as well as having associations with destiny, they are an appropriate choice.

She also makes use of a number of well-chosen **similes** to help in her descriptions, such as Victor's reference to Elizabeth – **'The saintly soul of Elizabeth shone like a shrine-dedicated lamp in our peaceful home'** *(Chapter 2)* – or his final view of the creature on Montanvert – **'I saw him descend the mountain with greater speed than the flight of an eagle, and quickly lost him among the undulations of the sea of ice.'** *(Chapter 17)* The use of 'shrine' along with 'saintly soul' suggests

figurative language language that uses figures of speech such as metaphor, simile, personification, imagery, hyperbole, symbols, etc.

simile a comparison that states its purpose by using 'like' or 'as'

Elizabeth is a heavenly being and also the holy centre of the home, while the notion of an eagle in flight gives a kind of nobility to the creature as well as superhuman speed. The creature himself uses a similar description when he tells Victor of his rejection by the cottagers: '**I was like a wild beast that had broken the toils; destroying the objects that obstructed me, and ranging through the wood with a stag-like swiftness.**' *(Chapter 16)* The idea of 'wild beast', 'broken toils' and 'destroying objects' is modified by 'stag-like swiftness', which implies an animal that is hunted rather than hunter. Since the creature is both at different times, the image is suitable.

Another of Shelley's descriptive techniques is the use of **metaphor**, e.g. when Victor says, '**the fangs of remorse tore my bosom, and would not forego their hold**' *(Chapter 8)*. This comparison of remorse with a snake is again appropriate if we consider the idea of Victor as Adam, who was tempted by the serpent and Eve to gain forbidden knowledge and suffered as a result. Victor also compares himself to the oak tree he witnessed being struck by lightning: '**But I am a blasted tree; the bolt has entered my soul**' *(Chapter 19)*. Again the metaphor is well chosen since it was this event that started his obsession with electrochemistry.

Mary Shelley's use of **imagery** is poetic and influenced by the Romantic notions of scenery and Nature and their influence on human feelings. She has Henry Clerval describe the peaks in Switzerland – '**the snowy mountains descend almost perpendicularly to the water, casting black and impenetrable shades**' *(Chapter 18)* – which uses the contrast of white and black to suggest the drama of the Alps and the effect of gloom they can create. When Victor is alone on his Scottish island, the dreadful nature of his task is emphasized by the place itself: '**The soil was barren, scarcely affording pasture for a few miserable cows, and oatmeal for its inhabitants**' *(Chapter 19)*.

The author uses **hyperbole** as a means of emphasis in her characters' narratives. Robert Walton says his lieutenant '**is a man of wonderful courage and enterprise; he is madly desirous of glory... retains some of the noblest endowments of humanity**' *(Letter 2)*. This exaggerated portrait tells his sister that, in spite of all this, Walton cannot see him as a friend. Victor uses hyperbole frequently, claiming, '**No human being could have passed a happier childhood than myself**' *(Chapter 2)* and later, '**A fiend had snatched from me every hope of future happiness: no creature had ever been so miserable as I was; so frightful an event is single in the history of man**' *(Chapter 23)*. These claims tell us more about the self-centred character of Victor than they do about the real nature of the events. The creature also uses exaggerated language to express his feelings. When he has just killed William he says, '**I gazed on my victim, and my heart swelled with exultation and hellish triumph**' *(Chapter 16)*. Following the rest of his tale, this surprising emphasis on revenge rather than his desire for acceptance tells the reader how much he has changed.

hyperbole exaggeration for the sake of emphasis

imagery a description that creates an image or picture in the reader's mind

metaphor a comparison that uses another thing, idea or action to suggest a likeness

Activity 7

a) Look at the following examples of figurative language from the novel. Discuss what figures of speech are being used, how appropriate you consider them and why Mary Shelley has used them.

- **The cup of life was poisoned for ever; and although the sun shone upon me… I saw around me nothing but a dense and frightful darkness, penetrated by no light but the glimmer of two eyes that glared upon me.** *(Chapter 21)*

- **Like Adam, I was apparently united by no link to any other being in existence… Many times I considered Satan as the fitter emblem of my condition; for often, like him, when I viewed the bliss of my protectors, the bitter gall of envy rose within me.** *(Chapter 15)*

- **The storm appeared to approach rapidly…** *(Chapter 7)*

- **I could not sustain the horror of my situation; and when I perceived that the popular voice, and the countenances of the judges, had already condemned my unhappy victim, I rushed out of the court in agony.** *(Chapter 8)*

- **Ruined castles hanging on the precipices of piny mountains; the impetuous Arve, and cottages every here and there peeping forth from among the trees, formed a scene of singular beauty.** *(Chapter 9)*

b) Write one or two paragraphs about Mary Shelley's use of figurative language, based on the above quotations or others of your choice. Give your views about its effect on the reader.

Writing about language

Upgrade

Examiners are often disappointed that students do not write in enough detail about an author's use of language. It is very important, whatever you are asked to focus on in your exam question, that you include discussion of a writer's style and techniques in some depth, supported by references and short quotations from the text. For example, it is not enough to comment on narratives in the novel. You need to show how Mary Shelley has chosen to enclose multiple narratives within each other and how this creates a distancing effect that lends credibility to the story as well enabling a comparison of the narrators. You should comment in detail, using short examples.

The outsider

All three of Mary Shelley's narrators can be seen as outsiders. The creature is the obvious one because his appearance means he can never hope to fit into normal society. He is enormous and apparently so ugly that nobody can look at him without suffering an extreme reaction. Even his creator, who worked on him for months, is appalled by his looks and runs from him. This first rejection by the man who should be responsible for him sets the pattern for everyone else who meets the creature. His looks make him an outcast before he has a chance to speak or act. The reaction of the shepherd is typical, as he **'shrieked loudly, and, quitting the hut, ran across the fields with a speed of which his debilitated form hardly appeared capable'** *(Chapter 11)*. The villagers too behave in a most unwelcoming way as **'some fled, some attacked me, until, grievously bruised by stones and many other kinds of missile weapons, I escaped to the open country'** *(Chapter 11)*. This makes the creature wary of being seen by humans and is the reason he doesn't want to approach the De Lacey family.

From his hiding place in the shed adjoining the De Lacey cottage, the creature gets to know the family. He notices the kind way in which they treat each other and the way they share things, whether good or bad, and this makes him aware of his loneliness. He tries to share their lives by helping them with chores, such as chopping wood and clearing snow. He realizes how different he is when, having admired their appearance and behaviour, he catches sight of his own reflection: **'... how was I terrified, when I viewed myself in a transparent pool!'** *(Chapter 12)* His conviction that he is a monster fills him with **'bitterest sensations of despondence and mortification'** *(Chapter 12)*. The creature works hard to learn the cottagers' language as Felix teaches Safie. This enables him to read Victor's account of his creation in the papers he finds in the pocket of Victor's coat. **"Accursed creator! Why did you form a monster so hideous that even you turned from me in disgust?"** *(Chapter 15)*

The De Laceys' rejection is a terrible lesson for the creature – that even those who seem to have more elevated thoughts and behave kindly to other humans will make no allowances for him. When he discovers that they have quit the cottage in fear, he feels they **'had broken the only link that held me to the world'** *(Chapter 16)*. He is filled alternately with anguish and fury, and revenges himself by burning down their cottage. It seems that, if they cannot accept him, there is nothing left. His desire for revenge on the human race is reinforced when his rescue of a young girl from drowning is misinterpreted and he is shot and left in agony.

Mary Shelley, through the creature's own story, suggests that he is drawn towards goodness and kindness until the prejudice shown towards him turns his feelings to revenge and hatred.

"I am malicious because I am miserable. Am I not shunned and hated by all mankind? You, my creator, would tear me to pieces, and triumph; remember that, and tell me why I should pity man more than he pities me?" *(Chapter 17)*

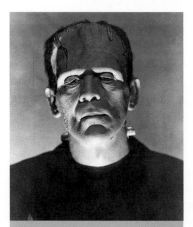

The creature's appearance alone marks him out as an outsider, as played here by Boris Karloff in the 1931 film *Frankenstein*

If the creature is an outsider through no fault of his own, both Robert Walton and Victor Frankenstein are outsiders by choice and their own actions. Victor has a loving family and friends whom he chooses to ignore in order to pursue the **chimera** of bestowing life: '**I wished, as it were, to procrastinate all that related to my feelings of affection until the great object, which swallowed up every habit of my nature, should be completed.**' *(Chapter 4)* This obsessive behaviour culminates in the 'catastrophe' of the creature's being. Once brought to life, either Victor must acknowledge his success and be responsible for his 'child', or he must reject his failed experiment, although without being able to destroy the result. He chooses the latter course and is then burdened with the secret knowledge of what he has done. He tells nobody, not even Henry Clerval: '**I could never persuade myself to confide to him that event which was so often present to my recollection, but which I feared the detail to another would only impress more deeply**' *(Chapter 6)*. Victor is lying even to himself by suggesting that telling his secret would make it harder to bear. This secrecy becomes a habit and it cuts Victor off from society, his friend, his family and his fiancée. It makes him an outcast in his own mind, afraid of what will happen if he confesses, even to the extreme point where he allows Justine Moritz to be hanged rather than tell the truth that will save her. After that cowardly act, the likelihood of confession becomes ever more remote. Victor retreats into himself, leaving his family behind as he travels to Chamonix.

chimera something hoped for but an illusion

His meeting with the creature on the ice plain shows the reader that these two outsiders have more in common with each other than with the rest of humanity, although Victor remains firmly in denial of this until all his loved ones are dead. Only with each other can they be honest since both know the truth. When, in a rare moment of compassion, Victor agrees to create a mate for his creature, he cuts himself off still further from those he loves, needing secrecy for his task. Developments of learning in Natural Philosophy take him to England in the company of Henry Clerval. However Victor still doesn't tell Henry the truth and Henry dies without knowing that his murder is Victor's responsibility. Frankenstein's abortion of the creature's mate results in his becoming a social outcast when he is arrested for killing Henry.

Once freed and in better health, he travels home in the company of his father, with the creature's words, **"I will be with you on your wedding-night"** *(Chapter 20)*, ringing in his ears. Victor is so egocentric he believes the creature's threat is directed only at himself and he arms himself for protection, leaving Elizabeth, who is the real target, ignorant and unprotected. His own perception of his outsider/victim status leads to the death of his wife. He does not consider confiding his secret to her until after they are married, when it will be too late for her to draw back.

Not until Elizabeth's murder, closely followed by his father's death, does Victor acknowledge the link between himself and his creation. Now a true outcast, spurred on only by the desire for revenge, Victor pursues the creature round the globe until they meet again, once more on a vast sea of ice. Only the third outsider, Walton, hears the full story from Victor and from the creature.

Robert Walton is an outsider by virtue of being an explorer with a burning ambition to find the North Pole and discover the secret of magnetism. A lonely childhood has left him without friends, which may explain his affection for his sister as well as his longing for a friend. When he finds such a friend in Victor Frankenstein, it is only to lose him again and to be forced into abandoning his ambitious voyage by the crew's insistence on returning home. While Victor dies, and the creature announces his intention of killing himself on a sacrificial pyre, Walton, the main storyteller, is left to return home, like the Ancient Mariner, and tell the story we have just read.

Other outsiders in the novel include the De Lacey family, who have been exiled from their native France by political enmity. The creature notes their difference from the local peasants because of their aristocratic ways and superior learning. Within their story is Safie, also an outsider by virtue of her Turkish background, although she is a Christian, unlike her Muslim father. Once they have served their purpose of giving the creature an education and showing that basic prejudice is common to all humans, the De Lacey family is written out of the story.

> **Key quotations**
>
> My rage is unspeakable when I reflect that the murderer, whom I have turned loose upon society, still exists. ... I have but one resource; and I devote myself, either in my life or death, to his destruction. *(Chapter 23)*
>
> Must I then lose this admirable being? I have longed for a friend; I have sought one who would sympathise with and love me. Behold, on these desert seas I have found such a one; but, I fear, I have gained him only to know his value, and lose him. *(Chapter 24)*

Prejudice

Connected with the idea of the outsider is the notion of prejudice. The creature's appearance creates instant prejudice in those who see him, partly through fear and partly because of the association of ugliness with evil and beauty with goodness. Stories such as 'Beauty and the Beast' tap into this association and Mary Shelley uses it in her novel. The creature only wishes to be accepted and to find out where he comes from. The fact that he has no name emphasizes his position as an aberration. The confirmation of his inhuman status, which comes from reading Victor's papers, added to his experience of constant rejection, drives him into misery and rage against his creator. As he tells the old Mr De Lacey, **'a fatal prejudice clouds their eyes, and where they ought to see a feeling and kind friend, they behold only a detestable monster'** *(Chapter 16)*. He finally succumbs to the prejudice against him and requests a companion 'of the same species', implying that he has accepted his inhuman status. His desire for a female companion is seen as reasonable, even by Victor, until he begins to reflect on the consequences for future generations of making her. Victor's own prejudice leads him to destroy the creature's mate, despite his promise.

Unlike the creature, the Frankenstein family are all good looking, as are Henry Clerval and Justine Moritz. Robert Walton sings Victor's praises: **'He is so gentle, yet so wise; his mind is so cultivated; and when he speaks, although his words are culled with the choicest art, yet they flow with rapidity and unparalleled eloquence.'** *(Letter 4)* However, the reader may rapidly draw their own conclusions about Victor's wisdom and gentleness when he tells his story. Walton's own prejudice is shown in his reference to Victor as a 'divine wanderer', excusable only by his desperate want of a friend of his own intellectual and social standing. On the other hand, while admiring the worth of his ship's master, he comments, **'but then he is wholly uneducated: he is as silent as a Turk, and a kind of ignorant carelessness attends him'** *(Letter 2)*. Clearly Walton does not regard the man as his equal, regardless of his noble actions.

Victor is prejudiced against his own creation, based on its appearance and its later murderous behaviour, but without considering the causes. He is also a snob and his class prejudice shows clearly throughout his narration. One of the first things he tells us is: **'I am by birth a Genevese; and my family is one of the most distinguished of that republic.'** *(Chapter 1)* He points out that Henry Clerval's father was 'a narrow-minded trader' *(Chapter 3)*. Similarly he tells us that Elizabeth's father was 'a Milanese nobleman', unlike her Italian foster brothers and sisters *(Chapter 1)*. Money seems to be no problem for Victor, as he hires carriages and boats, spends money on scientific equipment, and lives as he wishes without the need for a job. His creature, on the other hand, has only whatever he can forage and lives mainly on nuts, roots and berries.

Even the creature has prejudices, making distinctions between the cottagers and others: **'The gentle manners and beauty of the cottagers greatly endeared them to me: when they were unhappy, I felt depressed; when they rejoiced, I sympathised in their joys. I saw few human beings besides them; and if any other happened to enter the cottage, their harsh manners and rude gait only enhanced to me the superior accomplishments of my friends.'** *(Chapter 12)* It is significant that the author presents the creature himself as being influenced by appearances and behaviour as much as those who judge him in the same manner.

When Victor arrives in Ireland, he too is the victim of prejudice, as a stranger. He is seized by the villagers and arrested for the murder of Clerval on little evidence. He is fortunate that Mr Kirwin, the magistrate, is more open-minded than his countrymen.

Justine Moritz is another victim of prejudice, since she is disbelieved by the jury and bullied by the priest into a false confession. Nobody considers that the evidence, which Elizabeth states to be unlikely proof, may have been planted and the justice system, which Alphonse Frankenstein complacently relies on, is shown to be incapable of reaching the truth or dispensing justice. As Elizabeth comments, "Alas! **Victor, when falsehood can look so like the truth, who can assure themselves of certain happiness?"** *(Chapter 9)*

Key quotations

This man, whose name was Beaufort, was of a proud and unbending disposition, and could not bear to live in poverty and oblivion in the same country where he had formerly been distinguished for his rank and magnificence. *(Chapter 1)*

Activity 2

a) Discuss or consider how the following quotations show prejudice in the novel:

- **M. Krempe was a little squat man, with a gruff voice and a repulsive countenance…** *(Chapter 3)*

- **… when the man saw me draw near, he aimed a gun, which he carried, at my body, and fired.** *(Chapter 16)*

- **She was a hired nurse, the wife of one of the turnkeys, and her countenance expressed all those bad qualities which often characterise that class.** *(Chapter 21)*

- **What a glorious creature must he have been in the days of his prosperity, when he is thus noble and godlike in ruin! He seems to feel his own worth, and the greatness of his fall.** *(Chapter 24)*

What do you think Mary Shelley is trying to suggest about prejudice?

b) Prepare a one-minute talk on how prejudice is shown in *Frankenstein* and its effects.

The uses of knowledge

The search for knowledge is an important theme within the novel. Walton's quest for the location of the North Pole and the cause of magnetism is paralleled by Victor's obsession with finding the origin of life. Walton is doomed to fail because of his reliance on his crew, who refuse to venture further after being trapped in ice for several weeks. Frankenstein succeeds, only to spend the rest of his life bitterly regretting it. The creature's search for knowledge is a more modest affair, consisting only of becoming literate and articulate, in which he succeeds, only to discover that his learning will never compensate for his appearance.

Walton's ambition to **'sacrifice my fortune, my existence, my every hope, to the furtherance of my enterprise'** *(Letter 4)* is the spur for Victor to tell his own story as a warning against overreaching oneself in the pursuit of knowledge. Walton is not only risking his own life and fortune, but the lives of his men, and this consideration has at least occurred to him. His objective is to **'satiate my ardent curiosity with the sight of a part of the world never before visited, and may tread a land never before imprinted with the foot of man'** *(Letter 1)*. He dedicates himself to this ambition and considers he deserves **'to accomplish some great purpose'** *(Letter 1)*. In the end he announces his return, **'I come back ignorant and disappointed.'** *(Chapter 24)* The pursuit of knowledge may involve risks that others on whom you depend do not consider worthwhile.

Victor, meanwhile, is recounting how **'natural philosophy, and particularly chemistry, in the most comprehensive sense of the term, became nearly my sole occupation'** *(Chapter 4)*. Having overtaken his teachers in a relatively short time, Victor then pursues his own studies and experiments in secret. His failure to share the discovery he has made even with his teachers and then to use it in a manner that can only be considered against Nature is what brings disaster. Like Adam, he receives knowledge that might be considered 'forbidden'. Unlike Adam, he has a choice about what to do with it: **'When I found so astonishing a power placed within my hands, I hesitated a long time concerning the manner in which I should employ it.'** *(Chapter 4)*

This concept of knowledge as power may partly explain Victor's reluctance to share his discovery. This would not be consistent with his view of himself as the 'creator and source' of a new species. This image of himself as a divine authority takes over from the scientific curiosity that led him to make the discovery and it gives rise to the popular image of the 'mad scientist' acting as God. Although he sees himself as breaking the barriers between life and death and acting to **'pour a torrent of light into our dark world'** *(Chapter 4)*, the result is the opposite. The creation he rejects brings instead darkness, death and misery.

The creature, in the midst of his education by Felix, reflects, **'Of what a strange nature is knowledge! It clings to the mind, when it has once seized on it, like a lichen on the rock.'** *(Chapter 13)* This seems to be his way of saying that once we have learned something we cannot 'unknow' it, even if we want to. The creature's knowledge makes him unhappy because the more he learns about the society around him, the more he realizes he can never be a part of it. He has no family or friends, money or possessions and his hideous appearance cuts him off. His knowledge makes him eloquent, but in the end this is of little use to him.

Once able to read, the creature discovers the truth of his own creation from Victor's notes

---

Key quotations

Learn from me, if not by my precepts, at least by my example, how dangerous is the acquirement of knowledge, and how much happier that man is who believes his native town to be the world, than he who aspires to become greater than his nature will allow. *(Chapter 4)*

Activity 3

Discuss the following propositions about Mary Shelley's position on searching for knowledge:

- Some knowledge is too dangerous for humans and should be left alone.
- Knowledge in itself is not dangerous, but it can be misused in a way that brings hazards.
- Sometimes ignorance is better than knowledge, if we wish to be happy.
- Knowledge brings power but not wisdom.

Decide which of the above are relevant to *Frankenstein* and find examples and quotations to support them.

Language and communication

Language is seen as an important tool in the novel, both in the way it is used and in the way it fails. All three of Mary Shelley's narrators are fluent with language, even when they claim that words fail them. We can see from Walton's letters that he is very well able to describe his surroundings, his crew and his feelings in detail. He communicates his story to his sister while giving us a good idea of her reactions: **'Will you smile at the enthusiasm I express concerning this divine wanderer?'** *(Letter 4)* He apparently records the whole of Victor's story, although Frankenstein himself edits the account, which includes verbatim conversations as well as letters and the whole of the creature's tale.

Victor is described by Walton as fluent: **'when he speaks, although his words are culled with the choicest art, yet they flow with rapidity and unparalleled eloquence'** *(Letter 4).* Yet a man of such intelligence, who has the ability to use rhetoric to the crew even while dying, works in secrecy and silence on the greatest project of his life. It is Victor's failure to communicate, particularly with his own creation, that is partially to blame for disaster just as the rhetoric he uses to the crew has little effect on their desire to go home.

The creature does not initially possess language at all, like any newborn. He gradually realizes, by watching the De Laceys, that **'the words they spoke sometimes, produced pleasure or pain, smiles or sadness, in the minds and countenances of the hearers'** *(Chapter 12).* This makes him want to learn the language, but at first he can pick out only the names of objects and people. The idea of translation comes when he realizes that Safie uses a language that the cottagers do not understand. Since she does not understand them either, Felix teaches her French in a way that makes it possible for the creature to learn it too. He learns to read at the same time and his reading of Milton, Goethe and Plutarch makes him literate and eloquent.

The creature sees language as the key to his acceptance by humans. However he has no opportunity to use his hard-earned knowledge of language, since the sense of sight proves far more powerful to his 'protectors' and to all the other humans he encounters. When he does find an opportunity to use words, he is convincing and articulate: **'Believe me, Frankenstein: I was benevolent; my soul glowed with love and humanity: but am I not alone, miserably alone? You, my creator, abhor me; what hope can I gather from your fellow-creatures who owe me nothing?'** *(Chapter 10)* Victor tells Walton: **'He is eloquent and persuasive; and once his words had even power over my heart: but trust him not.'** *(Chapter 24)*

Mary Shelley uses the power of language in her narrators to change the sympathies of her readers. We may well accept Walton's estimate of Victor Frankenstein until we read Victor's own story. We may then feel sympathy for Victor, who has to endure the guilt of creating a murdering fiend, until we read the creature's story, which changes our feelings again.

Perhaps it is fitting that the last spoken words in the novel belong to the creature: **"My spirit will sleep in peace; or if it thinks, it will not surely think thus. Farewell."** *(Chapter 24)*

> **Key quotations**
>
> **Oh! my creator, make me happy; let me feel gratitude towards you for one benefit! Let me see that I excite the sympathy of some existing thing; do not deny me my request!**

Activity 4

In a group of four, play the roles of the De Lacey family after they have moved from the cottage. Imagine the conversation you might have about the monster who 'invaded' your cottage.

- What do you think old Mr De Lacey might say? He is the only one who actually talked to the creature. Base your comments on the dialogue in Chapter 15.

- How do you think the others might argue based on their reactions and what the creature overheard the next day?

Nature

In the Romantic tradition Nature is the guiding principle, especially Nature at its most extreme. The novel opens in the icy wastes of the Arctic Ocean, where it also finishes. Walton sees this land as pure, unpolluted by humans and, because unexplored, holding the promise of fame and endless possibility. Walton says of Frankenstein: **'The starry sky, the sea, and every sight afforded by these wonderful regions, seems still to have the power of elevating his soul from earth.'** *(Letter 4)* This spiritual reaction to Nature hides a different desire. From his

This painting by Romantic artist Caspar Friedrich in 1818 seems to show Man confronting Nature.

youth Victor tells us, 'The world was to me a secret which I desired to divine.' *(Chapter 2)* When he is 15, the sight of a lightning bolt destroying a tree incites his fascination with electricity. Later, at Ingolstadt, he is inspired to 'penetrate into the recesses of nature, and show she works in her hiding places' *(Chapter 3)*. He is aware that what he is doing can be seen as wrong and 'I shunned my fellow-creatures as if I had been guilty of a crime' *(Chapter 4)*. This transgression against Nature can and does end only in tragedy.

Victor comments at the end of his walking tour with Clerval, 'When happy, inanimate nature had the power of bestowing on me the most delightful sensations. A serene sky and verdant fields filled me with ecstasy.' *(Chapter 6)* This association of natural scenery with feelings permeates the novel. When Victor returns home after the death of his little brother he tells us, 'I contemplated the lake: the waters were placid; all around was calm; and the snowy mountains, 'the palaces of nature,' were not changed. By degrees the calm and heavenly scene restored me' *(Chapter 7)*. Similarly, after the death of Justine, when Victor retreats to Chamonix, the magnificent scenery is his main objective. Victor withdraws from society – even from his family – and spends more and more time alone with Nature, trying to find the healing which, too late, he realizes he has forfeited: 'the sound of the river raging among the rocks, and the dashing of the waterfalls around, spoke of a power as mighty as Omnipotence – and I ceased to fear, or to bend before any being less almighty than that which had created and ruled the elements' *(Chapter 9)*. Had he regarded Nature in this light earlier, he might have had more respect for her laws.

For the creature too, Nature is vital. Among his first perceptions are his natural surroundings: 'I gradually saw plainly the clear stream that supplied me with drink, and the trees that shaded me with their foliage. I was delighted when I first discovered that a pleasant sound, which often saluted my ears, proceeded from the throats of the little winged animals who had often intercepted the light from my eyes.' *(Chapter 11)* With the coming of spring, now that he has found the cottagers, he reflects, 'My spirits were elevated by the enchanting appearance of nature; the past was blotted from my memory, the present was tranquil, and the future gilded by bright rays of hope, and anticipations of joy.' *(Chapter 12)*

Once his expectations have been cruelly overthrown and he has sworn revenge on humans, the creature travels to Switzerland in search of Victor. He makes his home in the harsh terrain of the mountains and ice caves where he finally meets his creator. Victor's perception of the alps as 'sublime' is now forever haunted by the figure of the creature, appearing to taunt him with the death of William and later to mock his vow of vengeance on the graves of his dead family.

The creature, which came into being in a most unnatural fashion, becomes a child of Nature, clinging to precipices, bounding across ice fields and promising to exile himself forever, if he has a companion, 'to the vast wilds of South America' *(Chapter 17)*. He even swears by Nature: "I swear... by the sun, and by the blue sky of Heaven, and by the fire of love that burns my heart..." *(Chapter 17)*. Paradoxically his inhuman qualities – his size and lack of sensitivity to weather and food – enable him to fit into the natural world and to outmanoeuvre Victor in the final chase that ends with Frankenstein's death. The creature often leaves taunting messages on trees or cut into stone, using Nature as his writing materials.

The primacy of Nature is central to the story, rather than a mere setting. In going against the natural order and searching for the secret of life amongst death, Victor sows the seeds of his own destruction. He creates something that is hideous and frightening because it is unnatural. Only the arid wasteland of the Arctic can reflect the emptiness in Victor's soul. As Walton writes, 'I wish to soothe him; yet can I counsel one so infinitely miserable, so destitute of every hope of consolation, to live?' *(Chapter 24)*

Key quotations

The sight of the awful and majestic in nature had indeed always the effect of solemnising my mind, and causing me to forget the passing cares of life. *(Chapter 10)*

Activity 5

One of the ways in which Mary Shelley points out contrasts in her characters is through their views of Nature. Consider, or discuss, what the following quotations tell the reader about each character's feelings and approach to life:

- **It was the secrets of heaven and earth that I desired to learn** *(Victor Frankenstein, Chapter 2)*

- **The desert mountains and dreary glaciers are my refuge.** *(The creature, Chapter 10)*

- **Oh, surely, the spirit that inhabits and guards this place has a soul more in harmony with man, than those who pile the glacier, or retire to the inaccessible peaks of the mountains of our own country.** *(Henry Clerval, Chapter 18)*

Love and family relationships

Victor grows up apparently surrounded by a family that is close and loving and with a friend whom he loves and admires. There are hints that Victor's picture of an idyllic childhood are rather overdone. His father seems to find it **'necessary that he should approve highly to love strongly'** *(Chapter 1)*. This trait may be a clue about Victor's need to meet his high standards. We are also told of **'My mother's tender caresses, and my father's smile of benevolent pleasure... I was their plaything and their idol... to direct to happiness or misery'** *(Chapter 1)*. There is little mention of guidance or discipline except from Elizabeth, who has no position of authority. Indeed Victor specifically mentions a lack of explanation from his father when he shows him the novel by Agrippa, which his father dismisses as 'trash' after a careless glance. Naturally Victor continues to read and, in the absence of a guiding hand, **'was left to struggle with a child's blindness, added to a student's thirst for knowledge.'** *(Chapter 2)* On his way to University Victor reflects, **'I had often, when at home, thought it hard to remain during my youth cooped up in one place, and had longed to enter the world, and take my station among other human beings.'** *(Chapter 3)*

Instead, Victor withdraws more and more from his family, with whom he does not communicate, and from his teachers and fellow students. He still thinks of his father's words that **'any interruption in your correspondence (is) a proof that your other duties are equally neglected,'** but considers, **'my father would be unjust if he ascribed my neglect to vice or faultiness on my part'** *(Chapter 4)*. This suggests a guilty awareness that he was engaged in something his father would have seen as wrong. Even when he returns to Geneva, Victor spends less and less time with his family, although he sees their distress. It is as though he cannot bear to face them knowing he is responsible for the deaths of William and Justine. Nor does it seem he thinks their love will survive his confession of what he has done. He is proved right when his father dismisses his confessions after his release from prison as **'the offspring of delirium'** *(Chapter 22)*. Victor keeps silent most of the time although he **'would have given the world to have confided the fatal secret'** *(Chapter 22)*. Despite his involuntary outbursts, **'I could not bring myself to disclose a secret which would fill my hearer with consternation, and make fear and unnatural horror the inmates of his breast.'** *(Chapter 22)* Knowing his father's high standards, it seems more likely that Victor could not bear the disappointment his father would feel.

The creature sees the De Lacey family as a role model that seems to be ideal. They are loving and caring to each other, they bear their trials with grace and they are compassionate to those who ask for help. They are educated and enjoy literature and music. Despite all of these virtues they are not perceptive and compassionate enough to accept the creature, but take him only at face value and drive him away without giving him a chance to tell his story.

The creature's desire for love and companionship, having been spurned by his 'father' and then by his 'protectors', becomes centred on a companion like himself with whom he could live well away from humans. When this is denied him, he turns to destroying Victor's loved ones.

Robert Walton's family has some interest for the reader because his dying father made his uncle promise he would not allow Robert to go to sea – the one thing he really desired. Like Victor, he is engaged in exploration of a kind his father would disapprove of. The phrases he uses when writing to his sister seem to want her approval, while warning her of the exploration's dangers. His first sentence to her says, **'You will rejoice to hear that no disaster has accompanied the commencement of an enterprise which you have regarded with such evil forebodings.'** *(Letter 1)* From this we can infer that Margaret was not happy about his journey. He seems to swing between a desire to tell her everything and a wish to punish her a little by saying she may never see him again. By the end of the novel he has grown up enough to do his duty to her and the crew, and to tell his sister **'while I am wafted towards England, and towards you, I will not despond'** *(Chapter 24)*.

The love that Victor feels for Henry Clerval is paralleled by the love that Walton feels for Victor. Both recognize and admire what they see as moral virtues in the other and a feeling of like minds coming together. In both cases the loved one is taken by death, leaving the other grieving. Victor's marriage to Elizabeth, which has been arranged since they were children, seems rather pale by comparison: **"I love Elizabeth, and look forward to our union with delight. Let the day therefore be fixed; and on it I will consecrate myself, in life or death, to the happiness of my cousin."** *(Chapter 22)* The marriage is never consummated.

The concept of love and devotion between men and women depicted in the novel seems to reflect the society that Mary Shelley knew. Wives are mothers, nurses, comforters and self-sacrificing. They stay at home while the men travel and follow intellectual and physical pursuits. Victor's father goes to Milan on business while his mother adopts Elizabeth as a present for Victor. Victor goes to Ingolstadt while Elizabeth stays behind to run the household. Justine is called home to look after her hard, ungrateful mother and then returns to help look after the Frankensteins. Agatha De Lacey looks after the cottage and her aged father. The women seem to have little choice, but they are supportive, caring and devoted. These are qualities lacking in Victor, making him even more unsuited to usurp the role of 'mother'.

Key quotations

"What a place is this that you inhabit, my son!" said he, looking mournfully at the barred windows, and wretched appearance of the room. "You travelled to seek happiness, but a fatality seems to pursue you." *(Chapter 21)*

a) Mary Shelley did not have a happy childhood. Make notes on how she presents families, especially parents and fathers, in the following families:

- the Moritz family
- the Beaufort family (Victor's mother)
- the Clerval family
- the De Lacey family
- the Frankenstein family
- the Walton family.

b) Use your notes to create a presentation, either on a computer or a large sheet of paper, showing the part that family life plays in *Frankenstein*.

The divided self

Although the creature that Victor creates is portrayed as a monster, there are ways in which Victor himself is a monster, which may be why the two of them are often confused and called 'Frankenstein'. The monstrous part of Victor is his arrogant desire for glory, which leads him to follow a branch of knowledge, not for the benefit of people, but for his own gratification. Even knowing that his obsession is unhealthy does not stop him: **'Sometimes I grew alarmed at the wreck I perceived I had become'** *(Chapter 4)*. The coming to life of the creature causes Victor a severe mental and physical breakdown, from which he never really recovers – he cannot regain his mental health while he rejects his creation and leaves it to act as it wishes. He has no control over it because he admits no responsibility for it: **'This state of mind preyed upon my health, which had perhaps never entirely recovered from the first shock it had sustained. I shunned the face of man; all sound of joy or complacency was torture to me; solitude was my only consolation – deep, dark, deathlike solitude.'** *(Chapter 9)*

Victor knows that what he is making is unnatural and ugly: **'I had gazed on him while unfinished; he was ugly then'** *(Chapter 5)* but he is still taken aback by **'the filthy mass that moved and talked'** *(Chapter 17)*. Despite his aversion to what he has made, he is forced to acknowledge it: **'His tale, and the feelings he now expressed, proved him to be a creature of fine sensations, and did I not , as his maker, owe him all the portion of happiness that it was in my power to bestow?'** *(Chapter 17)* Victor, as the 'father' of this unnatural being, is joined to it and responsible for it. He is aware that this makes him as guilty as the creature of the crimes it commits: **"Justine, poor unhappy Justine, was as innocent as I, and she suffered the same charge; she died for it; and I am the cause of this – I murdered her. William, Justine, and Henry – they all died by my hands."** *(Chapter 22)*

Once the creature exists, Victor cannot unmake it. It is there inside his head, even when it is out of view. It appears in his beloved mountains and he knows instantly it is his brother's killer. This unwanted bond leads Victor to become more and more isolated just as his creation is isolated. Cut off from his family and friends by the deadly secret that he is just as much William's killer as the creature, Victor does not even attempt redemption by saving Justine. Instead he allows her to die and suffers a remorse that 'not the tenderness of friendship, nor the beauty of earth, nor of heaven, could redeem my soul from woe: the very accents of love were ineffectual' *(Chapter 9)*. Victor recognizes that the creature is a shadow of himself: 'I considered the being whom I had cast among mankind, and endowed with the will and power to effect purposes of horror, such as the deed which he had now done, nearly in the light of my own vampire, my own spirit let loose from the grave, and forced to destroy all that was dear to me.' *(Chapter 7)* The recognition only makes him more reluctant to confess because, he tells himself, it would be seen as 'the ravings of insanity' *(Chapter 7)*. He continues this false argument by reflecting that, even if he did tell them, they would never be able to 'arrest a creature capable of scaling the overhanging sides of Mont Salêve' *(Chapter 7)*. So Victor continues to justify his inaction and to suffer the consequences.

While Victor is compared with God the creator and Prometheus, the creature compares himself with Adam – although an Adam without Eve: "I am thy creature, and I will be even mild and docile to my natural lord and king" *(Chapter 10)*. The creature's comment is ironic in the light of what the reader knows. Victor's vainglorious attempt to play God has resulted in misery all round, including for his Adam, for whom he first agrees to create an Eve and then destroys her, using a similar false logic as his reasoning for leaving Justine to suffer.

Both Victor and the creature are identified with Satan. Victor tells Walton, 'All my speculations and hopes are as nothing; and like the archangel who aspired to omnipotence, I am chained in an eternal hell.' *(Chapter 24)* The creature, echoing his words, tells Walton, "the fallen angel becomes a malignant devil. Yet even that enemy of God and man had friends and associates in his desolation; I am alone." *(Chapter 24)* Victor and his creation are held together by mutual suffering and by the necessity for mutual destruction. The creature can be seen as Victor's

Creation of Adam painting on the ceiling of the Sistine Chapel, Rome by Michelangelo; the creature identifies with Adam, but should Victor see himself as God the Creator?

doppelgänger – the side of himself that he wishes to keep hidden and which he sees as ugly and sinful. However he has to acknowledge it, even if he doesn't want to, because it has an external presence that haunts him.

> **Key quotations**
>
> **"All men hate the wretched; how, then, must I be hated, who am miserable beyond all living things! Yet you, my creator, detest and spurn me, thy creature, to whom thou art bound by ties only dissoluble by the annihilation of one of us."** *(Chapter 10)*

doppelgänger a German word meaning a ghost or shadow of yourself

Activity 7

Mary Shelley presents Victor as obsessed with secrecy. He tells nobody of the creature until he goes to a magistrate after his father's death. This man does not believe him because he thinks he is mad. What motives does Mary Shelley give Victor for keeping quiet?

- He created the murderer so he is just as guilty.
- Subconsciously he knows he is bound to the creature more deeply than to his family and friends.
- He is aware that his rejection of the creature has caused him to become evil.
- It is his destiny to try and destroy the thing he has made or die in the attempt.

Discuss or consider these possibilities with reference to the text. Find examples and quotations to support your views.

Writing about themes

Upgrade

The way you approach themes in your exam will depend on the question you have been asked. You may be asked to focus on a particular theme such as prejudice, the outsider, Nature or the uses of knowledge. In this case you need to show how Mary Shelley brings out these themes in the novel.

Even if the question does not specifically ask you about themes, you should still show that you have understood them. For example, if you are writing about the creature, you could show how Shelley presents themes of the outsider, prejudice, love and relationships, and Nature.

You should also look at how the themes develop as the novel continues. For example, what happens to love and family relationships as the story progresses? Is the theme of Nature more, or less, important as the novel goes on?

Skills for the assessment

Understanding the question

Most questions will give you a published extract and ask you to use it in your answer. They will also ask you to refer to the rest of the novel to support your answer. You will be expected to refer in detail to the extract, quoting where appropriate. You should be selective in how you use the rest of the novel, making sure that your chosen references and quotations are relevant to the question. For example, if you are asked to show how Mary Shelley presents women in the story, then you should ensure that your references are related to women, rather than, say, the creature.

Try to approach the question in a business-like manner. Start by identifying what the question is asking you to do. That means underlining the key words and phrases, and noting what they mean. Examiners often use certain words and phrases; you can learn what they mean and that will tell you what you need to write about.

'**Explore**' means they want you to look at all the different aspects of something, so 'Explore the significance of family life' means you need to look at how families are portrayed in the novel; why families are shown as they are and whether they are important or not; what response is made to families at different places in the story; and how important family, or lack of it, is to the plot, structure and themes.

'**How does the author...**' or '**show how...**' means they want you to explain the techniques the author uses to gain their effects, so 'How does Mary Shelley make this episode tense?' means you need to look at how she builds suspense or tension in the way she structures the episode; how she uses language such as verbs and descriptions to make the reader feel excitement or fear; how she uses the reactions of the characters in the scene to make the reader see, hear and feel what they see, hear and feel.

'**Present**' and '**portray**' are similar words for looking at a character and mean not only what is the character like, but what devices does the author use to show us what they are like. So 'How is Frankenstein presented/portrayed?' means you need to say how he is described; what the author makes him say and do, and why; how the writer shows other characters reacting to him; and how the writer shows him as important to the story.

'**In what ways...**' means they want you to look at different sides of something, so 'In what ways are the scenes of Frankenstein's youth important to the story?' means you should examine how these scenes affect Victor himself, the effect on the reader and whether it gives you a greater sympathy with and understanding of Victor or not.

'**How far...**' means they want you to show the extent of something, for example, 'How far is isolation significant in the story?' Here you need to show the different ways in which Mary Shelley shows the effects of isolation on the three narrators in the novel. You should also write about how she portrays other characters who have family or social groupings and what this contrast suggests.

'**What role...**' means you are expected to write about not just the character and how they are shown but also what their function in the novel is. For example, 'What role does Robert Walton...?' means you have to write about his character and how it is shown but also about why he is in the novel at all. You would need to imagine the novel without him – he is an intelligent and ambitious man whose letters to his sister frame the story and whose similarity to Victor enables the reader to make comparisons between the two men.

'**Explain**' or '**comment on**' are phrases that invite you to give your response to something in as much detail as you can. For example, 'Explain the importance of the De Lacey family in the novel' means you should write about the way the family acts as an example for the creature and is responsible for his education. Without them, the creature would not know how a loving family unit works and he would have been left inarticulate, illiterate and unable to present his story.

Look at the question below. The key words and phrases have been highlighted and explained.

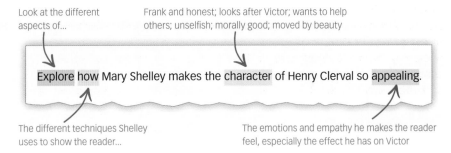

Look at the different aspects of...

Frank and honest; looks after Victor; wants to help others; unselfish; morally good; moved by beauty

Explore how Mary Shelley makes the character of Henry Clerval so appealing.

The different techniques Shelley uses to show the reader...

The emotions and empathy he makes the reader feel, especially the effect he has on Victor

You can see that you are being asked to do a number of things in this question. What you need to look at is:

- how Mary Shelley brings out the relationship between Henry and Victor
- how she shows the reader Henry's sympathetic qualities
- how she shows the opposite in Victor's egotism and obsessive attitudes
- how Mary Shelley makes the reader aware of the loss Henry will be to Victor.

Activity 1

Look at the question below.

> Explore the importance of Nature in the novel as a whole.

a) Highlight or underline the key words and phrases. Then describe what you are being asked to do.

b) Make a bullet point list of references and examples (and perhaps short quotations) you need in order to answer the question.

Activity 2

Imagine you are the Chief Examiner.

a) Write two or three questions that you think would test the assessment objectives for this part of the exam. Try to word them as they would be on an actual paper.

b) Swap with another student and analyse each other's questions as in the exemplar above.

Tips for assessment

Upgrade

To gain higher grades in the exam you need to show that you have thought about the novel for yourself and can give your own opinions about what the author is saying and how she is saying it, supporting your ideas with references and quotations.

Planning your answer

It is worth taking a few minutes to plan your answer before you start to write it. This means you will have the information you need in front of you and you will have some kind of structure. You will be free to concentrate on your writing style and making sure you have used the correct terminology and included evidence to support all your points.

Examiners always make the point that candidates who use their own ideas about the text produce fresher and more interesting answers than candidates who have prepared essays in advance. So the key is to practise planning answers to a variety of questions and, if you do want to write answers as practice, do not try to learn them by heart!

Look at the following question for planning purposes.

Read the extract from Chapter 10 that begins 'I performed the first part of my journey on horseback...' down to '... the habitations of another race of beings'. In this extract Victor is travelling to Chamonix to try and recover from his depression after Justine's execution.

a) Explore how Mary Shelley presents Victor's thoughts about Nature and feelings in this extract. Give examples from the extract to support your ideas. Ideas about Nature and creation are shown in this extract.

b) Explore how Nature and creation are shown elsewhere in the novel. In your answer you must consider:

- how Nature is related to creation
- how Victor considers this relationship.

The most useful thing about a plan is that you can jot down ideas quickly and then concentrate on writing your answer as well as you can. It is a good idea to use the extract as your starting point and write the main points in bullet points or as a spider diagram. It is best not to spend more than five minutes doing this.

You could make brief notes to the question above like this:

a)

- Nature means the natural world, such as scenery and weather, which has the power to lift Victor's spirits.
- In this extract he reflects on this power but doesn't seem to relate it to his own activities.
- Victor relates the Alps to 'another race of beings' – ironic since he meets the creature there next day (foreshadowing) – and calls them 'sublime'.
- Omnipotent power 'created and ruled the elements' = not Victor or science.

b)

- Nature also means the natural way of animal and human reproduction – overridden by Frankenstein
- The creature is 'a child of Nature' since he learns his first experiences from her
- All three narrators reflect on Nature and end up in the Arctic ocean – a metaphor for barren hopes
- Victor's main interest is in finding Nature's secrets – something he pursues in secret

A spider diagram on the same question might look like the example below. You could also add more bullet points or boxes in the form of references and quotations.

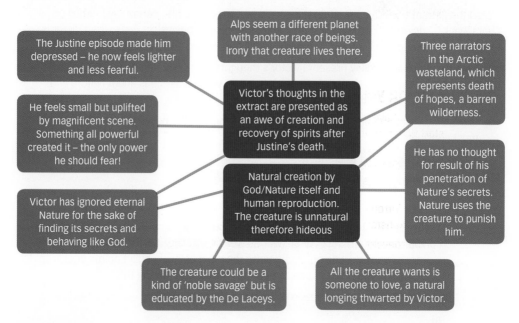

The Justine episode made him depressed – he now feels lighter and less fearful.

Alps seem a different planet with another race of beings. Irony that creature lives there.

Three narrators in the Arctic wasteland, which represents death of hopes, a barren wilderness.

He feels small but uplifted by magnificent scene. Something all powerful created it – the only power he should fear!

Victor's thoughts in the extract are presented as an awe of creation and recovery of spirits after Justine's death.

He has no thought for result of his penetration of Nature's secrets. Nature uses the creature to punish him.

Victor has ignored eternal Nature for the sake of finding its secrets and behaving like God.

Natural creation by God/Nature itself and human reproduction. The creature is unnatural therefore hideous

The creature could be a kind of 'noble savage' but is educated by the De Laceys.

All the creature wants is someone to love, a natural longing thwarted by Victor.

Activity 3

a) In a group of four, take one of the following questions each. Use either a spider diagram or a bullet point list to plan an answer to your question.

- Look at the extract in Chapter 4 beginning **'My father made no reproach in his letters…'** to the end of the chapter. In what ways does Mary Shelley show how Victor changes in this extract and throughout the novel?

- Read the passage in Chapter 12 beginning **'By degrees I made a discovery of still greater moment…'** to **'… such as *good, dearest, unhappy*.'** How important is language and communication in this extract and in the novel as a whole? Give reasons for your answer.

- Look at the extract from the beginning of Chapter 5 down to **'… shrivelled complexion and straight black lips'**. Consider the way Victor's animation of his creature and his reactions are presented. How well does this set the scene for everything that happens afterwards?

- Read the passage in Chapter 13 beginning **'Other lessons were impressed upon me even more deeply…'** to the end of the chapter. How does Mary Shelley present ideas about parenting in this extract and in the whole novel?

b) Share and discuss your plan with the rest of your group.

Writing your answer

Now you have your plan and you know what you need to write. Your structure should start with a brief introduction, develop your argument point by point, supported by references and quotations, and finish with a conclusion that does not merely repeat the introduction, but takes it further.

For example, in the question about the importance of Nature above:

- Your introduction might show the effect that scenery has on Walton and Frankenstein, and their views of Nature.
- Your development would show how the author portrays the way that Victor wants to make Nature's secrets his own, how he does this, and what the devastating results are.
- In the conclusion, you might say that Victor had learned a lesson about ambition which he passes on to Walton.

You also need to pay close attention to the quality of your writing in your answer, including your spelling, grammar and punctuation. Your answer should show your knowledge and understanding of:

- what the author is saying
- how the author is saying it
- briefly, how the setting and the context influence the writer and the reader.

Using Point, Evidence, Explanation (PEE)

Examiners want to see that you are able to support your ideas in a thoughtful way and that you have based them on what the writer says and means. For example, you might make the point:

> Once he has lost all his loved ones, Frankenstein thinks only of revenge on his creature.

Your evidence for this might be:

> 'But revenge kept me alive; I dared not die, and leave my adversary in being.'

Your explanation might be:

> This shows that Victor understands he must destroy his creature, for while it lives, it is a danger to humanity, and he cannot bear to think of it continuing when it has killed everyone he loved.

Tips for assessment

While it is helpful to use PEE as a guide, you do not need to follow it for every single point you make, only for the important ones, otherwise you may get bogged down rather than keeping your answer flowing.

Using quotations

This is an important part of using evidence in your answer. The examiner will want to see that you are able to select appropriate quotations that back up the point you are making. When you make a point ask yourself, 'How do I know this?' Usually it will be because of something the author has written – this is the quotation you need. For example, you might make the point:

> Victor is not interested in benefitting mankind, but only in personal glory.

How do you know this? There might be a number of quotations you could choose, but here is one:

> 'A new species would bless me as its creator and source; many happy and excellent natures would owe their being to me. No father could claim the gratitude of his child so completely as I should deserve theirs.' *(Chapter 4)*

By choosing this quotation, you will show several things:

- You can select a relevant quotation to support your answer.
- You have understood how Victor is blinded by arrogance and the conviction of his own superiority.
- You have understood that this relates to an important aspect of the idea of usurping God and Nature.

Examiners will reward you for using well-chosen quotations in your answer, but if you want to show higher level skills you will try to use 'embedded quotations'. These are quotations that are used as part of your main text, marked only by speech marks. Below are two examples of quotations as evidence – one is not embedded and the other is. You can decide which of them reads better.

> Victor treats Elizabeth as his own because that is how she is presented to him. '(I) looked upon Elizabeth as mine – mine to protect, love, and cherish. All praises bestowed on her, I received as made to a possession of my own.'

> Victor's mother gives Elizabeth to him as 'a present' and he takes this literally, even to the point of receiving any praise for her 'as made to a possession of my own'.

You can use this method for short quotations, which the examiners prefer as a rule. For example:

> When Victor beholds his creation he cannot bear to look at it and runs away. He does not for a moment consider what the creature's feelings might be, but only bemoans his disappointment that the dreams he had 'were now become a hell to me'.

Usually a brief quotation is all that is needed but occasionally you may feel it necessary to quote at greater length, for example where a shorter one would leave too much out or provide too little text to illustrate your point properly. If you really want to use a long quotation for some reason, then you would need to mark it off from the main body of your answer. Do be aware, however, that only one mark at most is likely to be awarded, whatever the length, so it's usually preferable to keep quotations short.

What not to do in an exam answer

✗ Do not begin with introductions such as 'In this answer I am going to show...'. Just start straight in and do the showing as you go. Make sure your introduction addresses the question and go back to it in your conclusion.

✗ Do not write lengthy paragraphs about the background to the novel. You may think that galvanism and electromagnetism are important in understanding the novel, but you should show this while you are answering the question itself.

✗ Do not focus on some parts of the set extract and ignore others. You should always answer on the extract as a whole.

✗ Do not write a long introduction showing what you know about the author. This should be a brief reference only if it is relevant to a point you are making. For example, you may think Mary Shelley's loss of her children had a profound effect on the way she presents Victor's attitudes to his creation throughout the novel, but mention this as briefly as possible.

✗ Do not go into the exam with a prepared list of points that may not be relevant to the question – and then write about them!

✗ Do not 'feature spot' in the set extract. There is little merit in saying that Mary Shelley uses symbolism without showing how she does this and what effect it creates.

✗ Do not run out of time to finish your answer. A plan will help you to avoid this.

✗ Do not try to write everything you know about the text – make sure you choose things that are relevant to the question.

Achieving the best marks

Upgrade

If you have read this section on Skills for the assessment, you will have some idea of the standard you need to reach to gain good marks in the exam. To reach the highest grades you will need to do the following:

• show an assured or perceptive understanding of themes, characters, setting and literary techniques

• show a suitable response to the text including appropriate use of subject terminology

• make sure your evidence is relevant, detailed and consistent, as well as integrated

• if required, make references to context that are appropriate and convincing, and supported by relevant textual reference

• write sophisticated and varied sentences; show good control of expression and meaning; use a full range of punctuation and accurate spelling.

You need to show that you have understood the novel on more than one level. On the surface, it is a story about how a scientist creates a monster that kills people because it is denied love. On an underlying level, it is a criticism of science that goes beyond what can be foreseen. It is also a critique of society and the prejudice with which it treats someone based on appearance. On another level, it is a novel about human and parental responsibility. Finally, it is a novel about good and evil and how we define the difference.

You will have to show that you understand the way in which the narrative works and why Mary Shelley chose to use three narrators. You will also need to show not just that you have understood the symbolism that Mary Shelley uses, but how, in your view, she applies it and why she uses it.

In addition you will need to use the correct literary terminology to make your answers precise and show that you have a sophisticated writing style.

Sample questions

1

Look at the passage in Letter 2 that begins 'I cannot describe to you my sensations on the near prospect of my undertaking…' down to '… unvisited regions I am about to explore.'

a) How does Mary Shelley present Robert Walton's character and ambitions in this extract? Give examples from the extract to support your ideas.

b) A desire to explore unvisited regions is shown in this extract. Explain how the desire to push the boundaries between what is known and unknown is shown elsewhere in the novel. In your answer you must consider:

- different kinds of exploration
- the results of the exploring.

2

Read the extract in Chapter 20 that begins 'I trembled, and my heart failed within me…' down to '… with a howl of devilish despair and revenge, withdrew.'

Starting with this extract, write about how Shelley presents the feelings and actions of Frankenstein towards his creation. Write about:

a) how Shelley presents Victor's behaviour as the person responsible for the creature's existence

b) how Shelley presents the importance of companionship in the novel as a whole.

3

Look at the passage in Chapter 24 that starts ' "Oh, it is not thus – not thus," interrupted the being… ' down to '… I am alone.'

a) Explore how Shelley presents the creature's fluency in his speech in this extract. Give examples from the extract to support your ideas.

b) Walton is one of very few people who allows the creature to speak. Explain how the creature relies on language to communicate with humans elsewhere in the novel. In your answer you must show:

- how people's reactions mean the creature has problems with communication
- what effects this has on the creature.

4

Look at the passage in Chapter 7 that starts 'We were soon joined by Elizabeth..' down to '… even after the sad death of my little William'.

a) Explore how Shelley presents the character of Elizabeth in this extract. Give examples from the extract to support your ideas.

b) Elizabeth's nature as a female is shown in the extract. Explain how Shelley presents Elizabeth and other women in the novel as a whole. In your answer you must consider:

- how Shelley presents women in the society of the novel
- why you think she presents them in this way.

Activity 4

a) Choose one of the sample questions. Make a plan for your answer, using a bullet point or a spider diagram plan.

b) Find another student who has chosen the same question and exchange notes and ideas.

Activity 5

Using the plan you made for your chosen sample question, choose one of the points you identified in your plan and write down how you would use PEE in your answer to show your skills in selecting and evaluating evidence.

Sample answers

Sample answer 1

Below is an extract from a sample answer by a student, together with examiner comments, to the following question on the novel.

Read the extract in Chapter 4 from 'Remember, I am not recording the vision of a madman…' down to '… greater than his nature will allow.' In the extract Frankenstein is describing to Walton how he found the principle of life.

Starting with this extract, write about how Shelley presents the importance of using scientific knowledge responsibly. Write about:

- how Shelley presents the attitude of Frankenstein towards his knowledge in this extract
- how Shelley presents the attitude of Frankenstein towards his knowledge in the novel as a whole.

Shows awareness of Victor's role as narrator.

Shows perception about Victor's motives; good use of integrated quotes.

In this extract Mary Shelley reminds us that this is Victor's narration and therefore we are getting his viewpoint on his activity, as we must because nobody else was there. He is anxious to reassure Walton that he is not 'a mad scientist' or fantasist but that his breakthrough was the result of patient procedures and 'the stages of the discovery were distinct and probable'. The breakthrough itself, which is 'the cause of generation and life' leaves him ecstatic, but seemingly with no desire to share his finding with anyone else. He uses his knowledge more like a secret weapon, gloating over the idea that he alone possesses 'the study and desire of the wisest men since the creation of the world'. This phrase is telling, since in Mary Shelley's time the creation of the world was still seen as the work of God, as was 'bestow(ing) animation upon lifeless matter', which Victor is now able to do. The suggestion is that Frankenstein now sees the possibility of his scientific power as equal to God's.

Shows very good understanding of Shelley's presentation of Victor's egotism.

Gives an intelligent evaluation of Shelley's use of language.

Victor realizes that he still has some way to go before he can use his knowledge to become a creator. He compares himself to Sinbad, the Arabian who was buried with his dead wife in the '1001 Nights' stories. He 'found a passage to life' by following a light. Frankenstein's symbolic light leads not from death as he imagines, but towards death and destruction. This is why he tells Walton that he will not pass on his secret because that would

Shows a good grasp of Shelley's use of symbolism and allusion.

result only in 'your destruction and infallible misery'. Mary Shelley gives Frankenstein's wish to prevent Walton following his example as the reason for his narrative. He wants to show 'how dangerous is the acquirement of knowledge' and he sees in Walton another version of himself. He is therefore anxious to demonstrate the appalling dangers of someone 'who aspires to become greater than their nature will allow'.

Thoughtfully compares Frankenstein and Walton.

Makes good use of appropriate quotations to support ideas.

The nature he refers to is his own. He wanted knowledge and the ability to 'penetrate into the recesses of nature' but without the temperament that could use it wisely. Had he confided his breakthrough to Mr Waldman, they might have decided how to use this power for good, but Victor's secrecy and determination to achieve personal glory will not allow him to do this. Instead he fixes his mind and energy on creating what he first conceives of as a human being and later becomes 'a new species', which he imagines will treat him as father–creator or God.

Intelligently explores the alternative possibilities rejected by Victor.

Makes a good point about Frankenstein's increasingly grandiose ambition.

Faced with the reality of what he has created, the disillusionment causes him to abandon his creation, along with his dreams, and refuse to take any responsibility for it. He has a severe breakdown, which is further proof of his unsuitability to handle the knowledge he was given and, instead of confessing everything to Henry Clerval, whose clear moral insight might have shown him a way out, he buries his head in the sand and hopes the thing he has made will somehow disappear. This unscientific and unrealistic attitude continues until he is forced to face up to the knowledge that his creature has murdered his little brother. Even this horrible fact does not force him to tell the truth and he allows the innocent Justine to be hanged, while prevaricating that nobody will believe him if he does tell his story, but merely see it as 'the ravings of insanity'. Since Mary Shelley has given us a man who clearly feels more sorry for himself than he does for Justine, we do not believe him and are more likely to see his reluctance as a desire not to appear a criminal in the eyes of his loved ones. He transfers his self-loathing to the 'fiend' he has created, vowing impotent vengeance on it, despite seeing that he, Frankenstein, was 'the author of unalterable evils'.

Makes a good point about Frankenstein's moral failings as reflected in his physical weakness.

Makes a very perceptive comment on how Frankenstein is presented as opposed to the way he views himself.

Makes a good psychological point implying Victor's need to use the creature as a doppelganger.

With the benefit of hindsight, Frankenstein can see that the knowledge he worked so hard for was beyond his capabilities as a person, but his self-deception remains with him until he dies. He tells Walton that he has been examining his past behaviour and 'nor do I find it blamable'. The reader may find this an

Makes a well-evaluated point about Victor's self-deception even near death.

Gives an intelligent analysis of the falsity of Frankenstein's logic.

Gives a thoughtful evaluation of Shelley's language showing Victor's innate prejudice.

astonishing remark in the circumstances, but Mary Shelley has already presented Frankenstein as an unreliable narrator. He is unable to see that his refusal to take responsibility for the result of his power makes him very blamable. He is still using false logic to claim that his agreement to make the creature a mate was right, but his decision to destroy it was even more right because his duty 'towards the beings of my own species' was more important. This is a phrase that acts as something of a giveaway, implying a prejudice that the reader may have sensed from the beginning. It explains much of Victor's attitudes and behaviour to his creature, but it in no way excuses it.

Overall this is a very thoughtful, intelligent and well-evaluated response. It shows a perceptive understanding of the theme of knowledge and how Mary Shelley presents it through Victor, demonstrating its dangers not only through his narrative but through his moral failings. It is illustrated with carefully chosen quotations and demonstrates Victor's role as an unreliable narrator.

Sample answer 2

Below is an extract from a sample answer by a student, together with examiner comments, to the following question on the novel.

> Look at the passage in Chapter 6 that starts 'We passed a fortnight in these perambulations...' to the end of the chapter.
>
> **a)** Explore how Shelley presents the importance of Clerval's friendship in the extract. Give examples from the extract to support your ideas.
>
> **b)** The nature of Clerval's friendship is shown in this extract. Explain how the nature of friendship is shown elsewhere in the novel. In your answer you must consider:
>
> - where and by whom friendship is shown
> - how it is shown and the effects of lacking friendship.

Victor and Henry have been friends since childhood and in the extract Henry is trying to make Victor feel better after his illness. They are on a walking holiday and the fresh air and exercise is helping Victor recover. He says that 'Clerval called forth the better feelings of my heart', which means that Henry knew how to bring out Victor's better nature – the side that wasn't obsessed with creating a monster. Victor says that Henry's 'gentleness and affection' made him feel warm inside and he found the happiness he used to have when he was a young boy. Henry teaches him how to enjoy nature again and 'the cheerful faces of children'. This may be an implied contrast to the 'child' he made and is trying to forget. Now he sees the spring flowers and green fields, and takes pleasure in the scenery again.

As his friend who really understands him, Henry encourages Victor and shows how imaginative he is by inventing stories 'of wonderful fancy and passion' to entertain him. Unlike Victor, Henry has no interest in science and is studying oriental languages and poetry, which he introduced Victor to as well. They helped to soothe Victor's troubled mind before the walking tour completes the job. Henry is shown to be just the sort of friend everyone would want. He nurses Victor when he has a breakdown after bringing the creature to life and spends most of his time trying to restore his friend to health and normality.

In the early part of the novel Victor describes Henry as a boy who likes brave and romantic tales of knights. He is Victor's only friend

Shows understanding of Clerval's motives.

Interprets an appropriate quotation correctly with some analysis.

Shows understanding of the effect of Henry's qualities, but without much evaluation.

Offers a good personal response, although it needs further explanation.

Gives a sound narrative response but this could have been related to Henry as a child.

Shows a fair knowledge of the novel and of Henry's role.

Gives a thoughtful response to Henry's dedication as a true friend, but could have gone further.

Makes a fair point about Henry's possibly restraining influence on Victor, which could have been more analytical.

Offers a perceptive idea that the friendship is definitely one-sided, which could have been expanded to include more than just 'secrets'.

This is true and shows good knowledge of the story. It could have evaluated Victor's motives in not asking Henry himself.

Makes a good point about Frankenstein's illogical behaviour where the creature is concerned.

Gives a valid personal response that could have been expanded. The association with breakdown could have done with more analysis.

Makes a neat conclusion to sum up the question, but could have gone further, perhaps by reflecting on friendship elsewhere.

because Victor is a bit of a loner who doesn't like being part of a crowd. It is a shame his father won't let him go to university as he might have stopped Victor becoming so cut off from real life. He might have prevented him from playing God as well, but by the time he arrives it is too late. This means he is still studying while Victor goes back to Geneva and sees Justine get hanged for William's murder, and while Victor has his conversation with the creature and promises to make him a mate.

While Henry is a good friend to Victor, it doesn't seem like Victor *is a good friend to Henry. Close friends don't usually have secrets from each other but Victor never tells Henry about the creature or warns him to watch out, even when it makes threats against people Victor loves.*

Henry travels to England with Victor and they go touring together, although this wasn't Victor's idea and it was his father who asked Henry to go, to keep an eye on Victor. Henry is interested in India and is planning to help European trade and colonization there, because he speaks some of the languages and has learned about their culture. Even though Victor says he wants to protect Henry in case the 'fiend' has followed them and wants *to get revenge for not yet having his companion by murdering Clerval, he then sends him to Perth alone while he goes off to the Orkneys to be on his own.*

The last we see of Henry is as a murdered body – the creature's revenge, not for Victor's taking a long time, but for him destroying its mate. *This seems a poor reward for the years he has stood by Victor and it sends Victor into one of his breakdowns.*

I think Mary Shelley is telling us that friends like Henry are *precious but that being a friend is a two-way process and you have to give something back, not just take all the time.*

This is a sound response, with some perceptive points and some personal response. It uses appropriate references and integrated quotations, but is lacking in much detailed analysis and evaluation especially in regard to the author's use of language and techniques.

Sample answer 3

Below is an extract from a sample answer by a student, together with examiner comments, to the following question on the novel.

> Read the extract in Chapter 13 beginning 'These wonderful narrations inspired me with strange feelings...' down to '... whom all men disowned?' In the extract the creature learns about human society, history and general behaviour.
>
> Starting with this extract, write about how Shelley presents the importance of moral behaviour in society. Write about:
>
> - how Shelley presents the creature's reactions to what he learns in this extract
> - how Shelley presents the creature's reactions to what he learns about human society in the novel as a whole.

The creature is eager to learn as much as he can from the cottagers but is puzzled by what he hears. He finds it difficult to understand how humans can be 'at once so powerful, so virtuous, and magnificent, yet so vicious and base'. This is a paradox that inspires 'strange feelings' in him. It is the beginning of his social education, as up till now, he has only had the De Lacey family as his moral example. Now he finds out there are people who can 'go forth to murder his fellow', a crime that the creature finds incredible – rather ironically, in view of his future actions. He discovers from these accounts why there is a necessity for 'laws and governments'. His sympathies lie naturally with the 'great and virtuous man' rather than with 'vice and bloodshed', which is Shelley's way of showing the reader how corrupted he becomes by the treatment he receives.

He also learns about social history and the way humans are divided by wealth and birth. He understands that one or the other is needed to gain respect in society, unless you wanted to end as a wage-slave, wasting 'his powers for the profits of the chosen few'. This is a very interesting comment on the part of the writer, showing her radical background, although it is the condition in which most of her countrymen languished. She presents the De Lacey family as impoverished aristocrats so they fulfil at least one of the conditions for respect.

Inevitably the creature applies these ideas to himself. He knows nothing of 'my creation and creator' but he is aware that he has

Gives a perceptive interpretation of Shelley's language.

Shows knowledge of the novel and understanding of the cottagers' role, which could have been developed further.

Gives a perceptive personal response showing awareness of Shelley's techniques, including the use of irony.

Thoughtfully uses relevant quotation and evaluates Shelley's presentation of the creature's gradual corruption.

Makes a intelligent point about context, showing understanding of Shelley's society and its influences on thinking.

Presents an argument well, which shows clearly how the author presents the creature's growing sense of identity and difference.

no money or possessions. He has an even bigger handicap – not only is he an outsider, but he is also 'hideously deformed and loathsome'. When he reflects on the difference between himself and the cottagers, being 'more agile', able to 'subsist upon a coarser diet' and to bear extreme temperatures better, as well as being far larger, he questions his identity. 'Was I then a monster. A blot upon the earth, from which all men fled, and whom all men disowned?'

Correctly identifies the 'turning point' in the creature's sense of justice and morals, with good analysis although further evaluation would be possible.

Although the answer would explain the prejudice with which he has so far been treated, the creature convinces himself that the De Laceys are different. The terrible disillusion that follows his discovery that they also regard him as 'a blot upon the earth' changes his moral viewpoint, leaving him no more in disbelief about what enables someone to commit murder. The only hope left to him is to find his creator, whose responsibility he must be, despite his rejection and hatred.

Presents an argument well, looking at narration and viewpoint, and evaluating fault and judgement.

Mary Shelley presents the creature's journey from innocent child of Nature to avenging killer through his own words, narrated, we must assume faithfully, by Victor Frankenstein to Robert Walton. He accuses Victor of causing the change by abandoning him in a most unparental manner. Even Frankenstein acknowledges he owes the creature the 'portion of happiness' that he was able to give, although his reneging on this decision causes a bloodbath of his loved ones. The only other narrator of his words and feelings is Walton – the only non-blind human to have wanted speech with him and who is touched by his grief at Victor's death.

Makes intelligent use of allusion and quotation to analyse a point about the creature's character and role.

Develops the argument about the creature's isolation and rejection, with a thoughtful personal response.

To him the creature reiterates his change from one 'whose thoughts were once filled with sublime and transcendent visions of the beauty and majesty of goodness'. He refers to 'Paradise Lost', the poem that had such an effect on him, by comparing himself to the 'fallen angel' who becomes a 'malignant devil'. The terrible knowledge of what he was and his eternal status as a lonely outcast has driven him to make his mark on society on the only way left to him. If they won't accept him, he can still force them to notice him.

This is a well-argued and intelligent answer that uses suitable examples and quotations to support its ideas. There is some thoughtful personal response and a perceptive understanding of the novel and the author's techniques.

Glossary

allegory a story with a second meaning, using abstract ideas as personified characters, behind the obvious meaning

allusion reference to another source that may be historical, literary or classical

anarchy a state without rulers where every individual has complete freedom; a state of lawlessness and disorder without rulers or laws

apostrophe a rhetorical device whereby an abstract thing or a dead person is addressed in order to give emotional emphasis

Archangel a northern port of Russia, at the entrance to the White Sea

aristocracy those with titles and wealth who owned large estates and stately homes, including members of the royal family

charnel house originally a storage chamber for bones at the time when graves were re-used; generally a place of death and decay

chimera something hoped for but an illusion

climax the event to which everything has been building

common land green spaces that were held in common by villagers who were entitled to graze their animals on them for free

Cornelius Agrippa, Paracelcus, Albertus Magnus medieval philosophers and alchemists

daemon originally a nature spirit, it later became a name for an evil spirit

doppelgänger a German word meaning a ghost or shadow of yourself

dramatic irony the situation where the audience knows something that the characters don't

elevated diction formal, high level vocabulary

figurative language language that uses figures of speech such as metaphor, simile, personification, imagery, hyperbole, symbols, etc.

foil a character that contrasts with another in order to show up certain qualities or failings

galvanism named after Galvani, a scientist who discovered the effect of electric current on dead limbs

gothic a literary genre that contains wild and picturesque scenery, melodramatic events which may be supernatural and an atmosphere of dread and horror

hubris a term from Greek drama meaning extreme pride and arrogance that leads to a character's downfall

hyperbole exaggeration for the sake of emphasis

hyperbolical Germanisms Scott seems to mean the more overblown emotional style of writers such as Schiller and Goethe

ice floe a large piece of ice that moves freely with the current

imagery a description that creates an image or picture in the reader's mind

immutable unable to be changed

inciting incident the event that leads to everything else in the story

Industrial Revolution the period when goods started to be made by machines in factories. It was brought about by the use of coal instead of wood, allowing steam engines to be used and iron to be processed more efficiently

landed gentry the social level just below the aristocracy, which owned local manor houses and smaller estates, and sometimes mixed with the aristocracy

metaphor a comparison that uses another thing, idea or action to suggest a likeness

Natural Philosophy the study of Nature through science that preceded modern natural sciences

omniscient narrator a storyteller who knows what all the characters are doing, saying and thinking

parable a story related to people's own experiences that illustrates a moral lesson often through personification and/or metaphor

Paradise Lost a long poem by John Milton that tells the story of the creation and fall of Man and of Lucifer/Satan

personification giving human attributes or characteristics to inanimate or abstract things

Plutarch's Lives the history of men who founded ideal republics and societies, both virtuous and vicious

protagonist the main character in a novel

resolution the way everything works out

rhetoric the conscious use of eloquence (fluent or persuasive language) to influence an audience

Ruins of Empire the central theme of this book by Volney is that empires rise when government allows enlightened self-interest to flourish

scarlet fever an infectious illness that mainly affects children and killed many in the days before antibiotics

simile a comparison that states its purpose by using 'like' or 'as'

symbol something that represents ideas beyond itself, as a flag is a symbol of a country or the colour white stands for purity

The Rime of the Ancient Mariner a long narrative poem by Samuel Taylor Coleridge in which the Mariner travels to the North Pole and is cursed for killing an albatross

The Sorrows of Werter a story by Goethe in which Werter falls in love and, in despair, commits suicide

OXFORD
UNIVERSITY PRESS

Great Clarendon Street, Oxford, OX2 6DP, United Kingdom

Oxford University Press is a department of the University of Oxford.

It furthers the University's objective of excellence in research, scholarship, and education by publishing worldwide. Oxford is a registered trade mark of Oxford University Press in the UK and in certain other countries

British Library Cataloguing in Publication Data

Data available

ISBN 978-019-836797-0

Kindle edition ISBN 978-019-836798-7

10 9 8 7 6 5 4 3 2 1

Printed in Great Britain by Bell and Bain Ltd., Glasgow

Acknowledgements

Cover: Mark Owen/Trevillion Images; **p10:** AF archive/Alamy Stock Photo; **p19:** United Archives GmbH/Alamy Stock Photo; **p26:** GL Archive/Alamy Stock Photo; **p27:** The Art Archive/Alamy Stock Photo; **p30:** The Art Archive/Alamy Stock Photo; **p31:** INTERFOTO/Alamy Stock Photo; **p37:** ZUMA Press, Inc./Alamy Stock Photo; **p40:** AF archive/Alamy Stock Photo; **p47:** AF archive/Alamy Stock Photo; **p57:** ZUMA Press, Inc./Alamy Stock Photo; **p60:** The Art Archive/Alamy Stock Photo; **p64:** AF archive/Alamy Stock Photo; **p69:** ScreenProd/Photononstop/Alamy Stock Photo; **p74:** ZUMA Press, Inc./Alamy Stock Photo; **p77:** classicpaintings/Alamy Stock Photo; **p82:** Peter Barritt/Alamy Stock Photo

Extracts are taken from Mary Shelley: *Frankenstein*, Rollercoaster edition (Oxford University Press, 2015).

MIX
Paper from
responsible sources
FSC
www.fsc.org FSC® C007785